Transi

Sheffield Hallam University
Learning and IT Services
Collegiate Learning
Collegiate Crescent
Sheffield S10 2BP

KT-215-351

101 815 629 1

eld Hallam University
and Information Services
drawn From Stock

DAY LOAN

Return to Learning Centre of is
Fines are charged at £2 per
No renew

Transitions in context

Leaving Home, independence and adulthood

Clare Holdsworth and David Morgan

Open University Press

Open University Press
McGraw-Hill Education
McGraw-Hill House
Shoppenhangers Road
Maidenhead
Berkshire
England
SL6 2QL

email: enquiries@openup.co.uk
world wide web: www.openup.co.uk

and Two Penn Plaza, New York, NY 10121-2289, USA

First published 2005

Copyright © Clare Holdsworth and David Morgan 2005

All rights reserved. Except for the quotation of short passages for the purpose of
criticism and review, no part of this publication may be reproduced, stored in a
retrieval system, or transmitted, in any form or by any means, electronic,
mechanical, photocopying, recording or otherwise, without the prior written
permission of the publisher or a licence from the Copyright Licensing Agency
Limited. Details of such licences (for reprographic reproduction) may be obtained
from the Copyright Licensing Agency Ltd of 90 Tottenham Court Road, London
W1T 4LP.

A catalogue record of this book is available from the British Library

ISBN-13: 978 0335 21538 6 (pb)   978 0335 21539 3 (hb)
ISBN-10: 0335 21538 6 (pb)   0335 21539 4 (hb)

Library of Congress Cataloging-in-Publication Data
CIP data applied for

Typeset by RefineCatch Limited, Bungay, Suffolk
Printed in Poland by OZGraf S.A.
www.polskabook.pl

SHEFFIELD HALLAM UNIVERSITY
WL
305. 242
HO
COLLEGIATE LEARNING CENTRE

Contents

Acknowledgements

The research material presented in the book is taken from an Economic and Social Research Council-funded award on 'The transitions out of the parental home in Britain, Spain and Norway' (award No R000238356). We would like to express a special debt of gratitude to Jackie Patiniotis, Sara Barrón López, Tor Erik Evjemo and Gjertrud Stordal for carrying out the interviews in this project and for helping us make sense of the very varied accounts of leaving home. We would also like to acknowledge the support of NTNU, Trondheim and the University of Liverpool in providing us with the facilities to carry out the research. While undertaking the project our thinking has been stimulated through various conference and seminar presentations and we would particularly like to express our thanks to Pat Allatt, Francesco Billari, Anna Cabré, Dave Featherstone, Janet Finch, Sue Heath, Gill Jones, Pau Miret Gamundi, Pete North, José Antonio Ortega, David Reher, Ken Roberts, Rachel Thompson and Bob Woods for their comments and hospitality, and to Berit Brandth for her thoughts on Chapter 2.

Above all, many thanks to the young people and parents who were so generous in giving their time, and for sharing their thoughts about, and experiences of, leaving home.

Introduction

My husband can't cope with our daughter's teen spirit

What you are describing is an inevitable and oft-repeated process, as regular in the scheme of things as leaves falling in autumn. Children are meant to grow up and leave home, and there are certain subtle processes happening to ensure they do. A certain amount of mutual repelling is inevitable, otherwise staunch family bonds might obstruct the thoroughly biological process of separation and dispersal.

(Margaret Cook, *Observer*, 8 July 2001)

Why study leaving home?

Leaving home has emerged as an event worthy of academic study in recent years, and there is now a growing scholarship around young people's experiences, both in contemporary and past times (Jones, 1995; Goldscheider and Goldsheider, 1999; Jurado Guerrero, 2001; Van Poppel et al., 2004). This growing interest reflects two observations about leaving home. First, that it is an event of interest in its own right and not necessarily something that happens as a result of other events, such as marriage or going to university. Even where it does happen for other reasons, the experience of leaving home is central to those events. Second, that as researchers gather more empirical data on leaving home it becomes increasingly apparent that individual experiences are extremely varied. Rather than leaving home emerging as an 'inevitable' process, as Margaret Cook describes it, it is the unpredictability of leaving home that is most striking. Yet our interest in this phenomenon is not just stimulated by the observation that 'it happens' or that individuals in different locations have varying experiences, but we are concerned with how leaving home relates to other aspects of young people's lives, hence our focus on 'home', 'independence' and 'adulthood'. It is clear, from some of the accounts presented in this book, that the process is of importance to the individuals concerned – both those who are leaving or contemplating leaving home and those who are left behind. The mere fact that leaving home is of importance to large sections of the population in several countries would itself be a justification for a socio-logical interest. However, the sociological interest cannot rest at the level of aggregate psychology. It is also clear that the leaving-home process is of considerable, and increasing, political importance. This is because of the numerous links made with other concerns, chiefly housing, employment and education, that emerge at this time. However, the fact of political significance is not a sufficient justification for theoretical significance, although it might provide some valuable pointers.

We start with the recognition that leaving the parental home represents a major life-course transition. Later, we express some reservations about the notion of transition but this can serve, at present, as a useful starting point. To say that it is a 'life-course transition' is to say that it is an experience shared by a clear majority within the population as a whole and that it takes place at around the same time within an individual life-course. As we demonstrate, this timing can vary between different societies or at different historical periods but the transition forms part of the common experience of indi-viduals within a given population. In conducting our research, we found few, if any, of our respondents who did not know what we were talking about or who queried the importance of the topic. And in talking about our research interests to colleagues or friends we found that most people had their own stories to tell. We also found that it was a topic that seemed to be receiving increasing attention in the media, which suggested to us that there were some special current issues in this topic over and above its seemingly timeless interest.

There are several additional points that we can make about this transition, which underline its theoretical and individual importance. The first is that it is multi-stranded and usually involves more than a simple change of address. The extent to which this transition represents a clear set or linked 'bundle' of different transitions (parental home to own home, single to married, educa-tion to employment and so on) has become increasingly problematic and part of the current fascination with the topic lies in the fact that these, and other, transitions can no longer be assumed to hang together. It can, for example, no longer be assumed in the UK that women leave home in order to get married. However, this does not mean that the leaving-home process has become sim-plified through the weakening of the connections to these other transitions. Rather, the process remains complex but in different ways and, if the process and the timing have become more complex, it is a key aim of this book to explore these complexities.

We begin our account of these complexities in Chapter 1 by reviewing the pertinent characteristics of leaving-home transitions in modern industrialized societies and how these are associated with differences by gender, class, education and labour market experiences. In Chapter 2 we outline the main theoretical debates that have stimulated our interpretation of leaving home transitions and the methodology that we have used in researching this experience in three European countries. In Chapter 3 we turn to the first of our substantive themes to consider how time and generation are implicated in leaving home. The very notion of transition relates to issues of generation and the life-course and the links between individual life changes and wider historical currents. Further, there are questions to do with the 'right' time to leave home and the ways in which this is negotiated or constructed in different social contexts.

As well as time, leaving home is clearly linked to the production of space because it entails not simply a move from one social space to another but the active construction of a new space, while remaining within the parental home also raises question of the production and the negotiation of space. Our focus on 'home' in Chapter 4 deals with these spatial aspects of leaving, or not leaving, home. In the course of our research and exploration of the relevant, and very rich, literature, we found that home was both a very complex and multi-stranded idea but also something which carried considerable emotional and moral force. A core theme of leaving home is independence, which we explore further in Chapter 5. Again, within modern society this is also a moral identity although, again, not one that has gone unchallenged. There are also links here to other themes of current interest, especially the idea of 'individualization'. Leaving home processes are associated with the achievement of adulthood. As we argue in Chapter 6, the idea of adulthood is a complex one and not one that receives universal or unqualified endorsement. However, there is no doubt that it represents an important moral identity, partly through the influence of developmental psychology and partly through its association with terms such as 'maturity' and 'responsibility'.

We consider each theme separately, but part of the interest of leaving home is the extent to which these three very important themes are inter-related and constitute some kind of coherent package. Thus it might be assumed that the movement from the parental home and the formation of an independent home are intimately bound up with the achievement of independence and the assumption of an adult identity. While it is clear that some people do make these kinds of assumptions in relation to their own personal transitions, it is equally apparent that for many people matters are much less clear or straightforward. The various ways in which these important themes of home, adulthood and independence are inter-connected constitutes a core concern of this book.

In thinking through these different aspects of leaving home it is evident that we are not simply dealing with an individual set of decisions or experiences but a process that involves inter-relationships and inter-dependencies with numerous 'others', and we conclude our study of leaving home in

Chapter 7 by considering how young people's lives are embedded in this way. Crucially, of course, the process involves the people who are left behind, chiefly parents and other siblings, as well as the individual making the move.

Leaving home often involves moving to live with other people who are moving through similar transitions, so we also need to think about impacts of partners and/or friends in destinations. Significant others may well also include other family members not located in the parental home such as grandparents and sets of friends. We also consider the significance of the 'generalized other' in the decision to leave home and its negotiation.

Finally, we may note that the leaving-home process must be considered in relation to a whole range of social divisions as well as those to do with age and generation. Clearly, issues of gender are implicated, although not always in ways that are direct or obvious. The whole leaving-home process is mediated through other social divisions such as those of ethnicity and social class. As issues of leaving home are so much bound up with the life chances and social and cultural capital available to any individual, it is not surprising that there are such inter-connections. At a more global level, differences in the processes of leaving home and the norms and values associated with it are also related to cultural differences between and within nations.

Most of our material is taken from a research project on leaving home, funded by the UK Economic and Social Research Council, which we carried out with young people and their parents in three European cities: Liverpool in the UK, Bilbao in Spain and Trondheim in Norway. In writing the book we have been stimulated as much by the concerns and issues raised by our respondents as by our own perspectives on leaving home.

1 Trends and patterns of leaving home

It is now becoming much harder to generalize about youth transitions, in terms of timing, synchronicity, causal factors and outcomes, as the concepts of individualization and risk have become central to the ways in which youth research has developed in recent years (Furlong and Cartmel, 1997). In the subsequent chapters of this book we follow this agenda in interrogating individual experiences in different contexts. However, while our overall agenda is more closely suited to qualitative approaches, we also recognize the contribution of quantitative techniques in accounting for overall patterns and trajectories of youth transitions and we begin our account of putting transitions in context by reviewing the characteristics of leaving home in different national and regional contexts.

A statistical review of young people's lives is informative in that it guides researchers as to the pertinent features of transitions in terms of timing and the relationships between different events (for example, transitions in employment, education and housing). Furthermore the increasing availability of longitudinal data facilitates more detailed analysis of how transitions differ for different groups of young people, distinguishing by characteristics such as sex, socio-economic background, education history and place of residence (Bynner et al., 2002). Longitudinal models are increasingly being used to develop causal models of transitions based on both individual characteristics and structural determinants, particularly labour market factors and social assistance programmes (Billari, 2001).

However, analyses of overall patterns and the causal factors that affect different trajectories and outcomes are not purely for academic interest, but help to give a sense of the context in which individuals negotiate their own transitions. Statistics come into our everyday lives. For example, the media provide us with snapshots of information about the statistical 'norms' of family life, while policy initiatives for young people will be based on a certain set of assumptions about their lives, such as the decision to set a lower minimum wage for workers below the age of 25 in the UK, which identifies a boundary line between being a 'young' and a 'fully independent' adult. As we explore in this book, young people often compare their own experiences and opportunities against an awareness of what 'other' people are doing. An awareness of average ages of leaving home, or of the common age ranges within which 'most' young people leave, contributes to the resources that young people might draw on in negotiating their own lives to obtain at least a vague sense of what is the 'right' thing to do and when is the 'right' time to do it (Settersten, 1998). Most of these comparisons are achieved through comparisons with family members and peers, but they can also involve a more abstract comparison with 'other people'. Part of the knowledge of 'other people' comes indirectly, through various media that provide 'models' of transitions, some of which young people might reject or embrace.

Leaving home in national contexts

Data on leaving home transitions tell an intriguing story about cross-national differences. If we randomly stopped young people in places as diverse as New York, Tokyo, Madrid, Oslo and London, we might be struck by the many similarities of youth in these cities, such as the clothes they are wearing, the music they are listening to, their opinions about citizenship and global events; however if we asked them if they lived with their parents, we would expect very different responses. As numerous studies have demonstrated (Cavalli and Galland, 1995; Holdsworth, 2000; Billari et al., 2001; Corijn and Klijzing, 2001; Iacovou and Berthoud, 2001; Jurado Guerrero, 2001; Aassve et al., 2002; Oinonen, 2003) the timing and the reasons for leaving home vary considerably between modern industrialized countries.

However, it is far from straightforward to document this variation as data on leaving home are not, for a number of very good reasons, routinely collected by national statistical agencies. There is no shortage of data on other transitions, such as age at marriage and age at first birth, a search for age at leaving home will generate far fewer returns. This can partly be explained by the fact that there is less official interest in leaving home, as in terms of understanding family formation patterns, marriage and fertility rates are more pertinent. It also reflects the fact that it is much harder to collect standardized data on leaving home. As we explore throughout this book, leaving home is rarely a one-off event, but is more appropriately treated as a process, often involving multiple departures and returns (Molgat, 2002). It is not, therefore, straightforward to ask young people the age that they left home. Researchers need to be able to take a consistent view on what constitutes a leaving-home event. This often involves taking the age that young people first left home, although care still needs to be taken in dealing with more temporary transitions, such as going to university, which some young people might treat as 'living away from', rather than leaving, home. Alternatively, although this practice might be less common in modern industrialized societies, some young people might never leave, but become the householders in their parents' home. This latter group will be treated in statistical returns as never leaving home, but that this does not necessarily mean that they defer the transition to independence and adulthood.

Notwithstanding these problems in defining what it is we are trying to measure with data on leaving home, in recent years increasing availability of both cross-sectional and longitudinal data has facilitated cross-national comparisons of the timing of this event. Cross-sectional data, such as censuses or labour force surveys, can be used to ascertain the proportion of young people living with parents (young people are usually defined as those aged 18 to 30, or maybe up to 35) and the median age of leaving – the age at which half of all young people have left (see Schürer, 2004 for discussion of the use of census data in historical populations). However, longitudinal data either in the form of retrospective surveys such as the Family and Fertility Surveys (FFS, see Corjin and Klijzing, 2001), or panel data such as the European Community Household Panel (ECHP, Eurostat, 2002), are preferable as they allow for more dynamic event-history modelling of the timing, synchronicity (Billari, 2001) and explanatory factors of leaving home. Event-history modelling or survival analysis is used to analyse events and their causes. For leaving home, we define an age at which young people become 'at risk' of leaving home (which can either be a chronological age such as 16, or related to other events such as leaving school) and model the causal factors associated with either early or delayed leaving, after this point of 'entry' into the model (Yamaguchi, 1991).

We have used published analyses of leaving home to compare median ages of leaving cross-nationally. Table 1.1 presents a summary of median ages for various countries in Europe, North America/Australia, Asia and Latin America. The data refer mostly to young people born in the early 1960s who left home in the 1980s. This time period has been chosen as it covers the cohorts included in the FFS, which have proved extremely useful for comparative studies of leaving home (Billari et al., 2001; Corjin and Klijzing, 2001). The data have been taken from a number of published studies of analysis of leaving home, including Billari et al.'s (2001) analysis of the FFS, which provides the most comprehensive analysis of comparative timings in Europe.

Median ages at leaving vary from 18.1 for women in Australia to 26.7 for men in Italy. In all counties, with the exception of Japan, women leave home earlier than men, though the magnitude of this gender difference varies from less than half a year in Slovenia to three and a half years in Hungary, with greater differences occurring in countries with older profiles. Concentrating on Europe first, the variation in timing of leaving is striking and, as Iacovou and Berthoud (2001) suggest, the timing of leaving in the West may be divided into a northern 'early' and a southern 'late' pattern. Billari et al.'s

Table 1.1 Comparisons of median age of leaving home

Country	Year/cohort	Median age: men	Median age: women	Data source	Study
Europe					
Austria	Cohort: c1960	21.8	19.9	FFS	Billari et al. (2001)
Belgium	Cohort: c1960	23.3	21.5	FFS	Billari et al. (2001)
Czech Republic	Cohort: c1960	23.8	21.2	FFS	Billari et al. (2001)
East Germany	Cohort: c1960	22.4	20.6	FFS	Billari et al. (2001)
Finland	Cohort: c1960	21.7	19.8	FFS	Billari et al. (2001)
France	Cohort: c1960	21.5	19.8	FFS	Billari et al. (2001)
Hungary	Cohort: c1960	24.8	21.3	FFS	Billari et al. (2001)
Italy	Cohort: c1960	26.7	23.6	FFS	Billari et al. (2001)
Latvia	Cohort: c1960	24.1	21.3	FFS	Billari et al. (2001)
Lithuania	Cohort: c1960	20.3	19.8	FFS	Billari et al. (2001)
Netherlands	Cohort: c1960	22.5	20.5	FFS	Billari et al. (2001)
Norway	Cohort: c1960	21.4	19.8	FFS	Billari et al. (2001)
Poland	Cohort: c1960	25.8	22.5	FFS	Billari et al. (2001)
Portugal	Cohort: c1960	24.3	21.8	FFS	Billari et al. (2001)
Slovenia	Cohort: c1960	20.9	20.5	FFS	Billari et al. (2001)
Spain	Cohort: c1960	25.7	22.9	FFS	Billari et al. (2001)
Sweden	Cohort: c1960	20.2	18.6	FFS	Billari et al. (2001)
Switzerland	Cohort: c1960	21.5	19.2	FFS	Billari et al. (2001)
UK	Cohort: c1960	22.4	20.3	FFS	Billari et al. (2001)
West Germany	Cohort: c1960	22.4	20.8	FFS	Billari et al. (2001)

Table 1.1   (*continued*)

North America/
Australia

Australia	Cohort: mid 1960s	18.6	18.1	HILDA	Flatau et al., 2003
Canada	Cohort: 1961–5	22.7	20.9	1995 General Social Survey	Statistics Canada
US	1970–80	21.5	20.8	Census	Yi et al. (1994)
Asia					
China	1982–90	25.0	23.9	Census	Yi et al. (1994)
Japan	Cohort: 1964–9	22.4	23.8	Third National Survey on Household Change	Suzuki (2001)
Malaysia	Cohort: 1958–67	24	22	Second Malaysian Family Life Survey	Johnson and DaVanzo (1998)
South Korea	1975–80	26.6	23.5	Census	Yi et al. (1994)
Latin America			Men and women		
Columbia	mid-1970s		23	WFS	De Vos (1989)
Costa Rica	mid-1970s		24	WFS	De Vos (1989)
Dominican Republic	mid-1970s		22	WFS	De Vos (1989)
Mexico	mid-1970s		23	WFS	De Vos (1989)
Panama	mid-1970s		24	WFS	De Vos (1989)
Peru	mid-1970s		25	WFS	De Vos (1989)

(2001) analysis also covers Eastern Europe and here the breakdown between north and south is less clear. Family historians have long recognized the significance of a east/west divide, following Hajnal's (1965) observation that for patterns of household formation a line could be drawn from St Petersburg to Trieste dividing the 'late' marriage pattern in the west, from the early and universal marriage system in the east. We might expect, therefore, that the timing of leaving home follows this pattern. However what is apparent from Table 1.1 is that there is no uniform pattern in eastern Europe, with timing varying from very early (Lithunia) to late (Poland). Even countries with common political and social heritage do not conform when it comes to the timing of leaving home – for example there is a difference of almost 4 years in the median age of leaving for men in Lithuania and Latvia.

Turning our attention outside of Europe we find more uniformity in geographical or 'cultural' clusters of countries. In North America and Australia median ages of leaving are comparable to those in northern Europe, although Australia has one of the youngest profiles. In contrast the timing of leaving in Asia is closer to that found in southern Europe. One country that stands out in particular here is Japan, which, rather surprisingly, has the youngest profile in Asia. This finding does not necessarily fit with stereotypical images of Japanese family life, which stress the importance of family solidarity and high levels of co-residence between adult children and parents (Budak et al., 1996). Suzuki's analysis offers a possible explanation in that what distinguishes the Japanese model is the high proportion of young people, especially men, who leave home to go to university. The timings of leaving home in Japan therefore follows a bi-modal distribution, with one younger peak associated with leaving to go to university and an older peak associated with getting married.

Once we move outside of Europe, North America and Asia there are very few data on leaving home. De Vos's (1989) analysis of leaving home in South America is one of the few case studies and was in fact one of the first comparative studies of leaving home. These data refer to a slightly older cohort, but they suggest that the South American pattern is closer to the southern European/ Asian model.

Destination

Identifying destinations on leaving is key to understanding some of the differences in timing, as some destinations, such as leaving home to go to university, are more common among younger leavers, while leaving to get married is associated with leaving at older ages. We therefore find that if we look at the living arrangements of young people in countries with different age profiles of leaving home, that the propensity to leave early or late equates to the proportion who are living alone, living with friends, cohabiting or married. Broadly speaking, in countries with older ages of leaving, transitions out of the parental home tend to be more 'permanent' and more likely to be for marriage. This is particularly the case in Europe, where Iacovou and Berthoud's (2001) analysis of women's partnership status in southern and northern Europe, which we summarize in Table 1.2, clearly illustrates that more women in the south who have left home are in marital unions, compared to their peers in the north who favour cohabiting.

The variation in being in a partnership reveals some interesting findings.

Table 1.2 Partnership status of women aged 21–25 who have left home, by country, early 1990s

	In partnership		Not in partnership
	Cohabiting Row %	Married Row %	Row %
Finland	52	22	26
Denmark	54	10	36
Netherlands	40	32	28
UK	32	41	27
Belgium	29	57	14
France	40	32	28
Germany	24	42	34
Austria	29	43	28
Ireland	14	38	48
Portugal	7	80	13
Spain	9	75	16
Italy	5	80	15
Greece	5	71	24

Source: Iacovou and Berthoud, 2001.

There is more variation in the proportion of women in different types of partnership compared to the proportion of women who are either in or not in partnerships. We do find, however, that more women in Ireland are not in a partnership than elsewhere, and generally more women in the south are in partnerships.

Table 1.2 illustrates the importance of partnership formation for leaving home, but among those who do not leave for partnership there are other important institutional practices. In particular, the transition to higher education is significant in that it either has a clear impact on accelerating transitions (as in the case of Japan) or delaying leaving home if most young people study at local universities, as is the case in southern Europe.

Generally we find that in countries with older profiles there is more homogeneity around reasons for leaving. In Spain and Italy for example, many young people 'delay' leaving as they are 'waiting' to leave under a certain set of circumstances, that is to live with (or marry) a partner. In contrast there is greater heterogeneity where the link between leaving home and marriage has been broken (Holdsworth and Elliott, 2001). We might regard leaving home prior to marriage as part of the destandardization of family life (Beck and Beck-Gernsheim, 1995), and data on trends would appear to support this. Data for western Europe for the latter part of the twentieth century clearly show a trend away from marriage towards either living alone/sharing or cohabitation. Even in southern Europe, where the dominant pattern is to leave to marry, there has been a rise in cohabitation in recent years (Kiernan, 2004). While cohabitation is more obviously part of this the destandardization of family practices, leaving home prior to marriage is not. If we take a longer historical perspective on leaving home, available data for the nineteenth century and earlier illustrate that leaving prior to marriage (and multiple departures) was common practice, particularly in northern Europe (Wall, 1978; Pooley and Turnbull, 2004).

Time

Despite the clear difference in timing of leaving home throughout modern industrialized economies, one trend that does appear to be almost universal is that in more recent years, in countries for which data are available, there has been an increase in the number of young people living with parents. For example Fernández Cordón's (1997) analysis of European Labour Force Survey data found that the proportion of young people living at home has increased significantly in Spain, Greece and Italy between 1986 and 1994, with smaller increases in France and Germany, although he found that the trend in the UK went in the other direction. The trend towards delaying leaving home is also replicated in Corijn and Klijzing's review of analysis of the European FFS. Outside of Europe the propensity to delay leaving home has been the focus of much debate in North America and Australia, although the extent to which this emerges as a key trend does depend on the historical timeframe used for analysis. The recent increase in the number of young people living with parents in Australia (Flatau et al., 2003) and the US (Gutmann et al., 2002) has occurred after a period in which the age of leaving home has declined. Median ages in both countries at the end of the twentieth century are commensurate with those at the beginning. Elsewhere the evidence of delayed leaving is slightly more complicated. In Great Britain, for example, there is an important relationship with age. In contrast with Fernández Cordón's finding, more recent data on proportions of young people living with parents do suggest an increase in living with parents (see Table 1.3). Murphy and Wang's (1998) detailed analysis of the BHPS also indicates a delay in leaving home in the late 1980s and early 1990s. However, Berrington and Murphy (1994) using cross-sectional labour force data, found that the proportion of teenagers not living with parents has continued to rise during the 1980s, but the leaving propensity of young 20-year-olds has slowed down. This pattern may be explained by increasingly fragility of early leaving, particularly if it is associated with transitions to higher education.

Table 1.3 Percentage of young adults living with parents: by gender and age, England

	1977–8	1991	1998–9
Males			
20–24	52	50	56
25–29	19	19	24
30–34	9	9	11
Females			
20–24	31	32	38
25–29	9	9	11
30–34	3	5	4

Source: National Dwelling and Household Survey and Survey of English Housing, DETR and Labour Force Survey, ONS

Explanatory factors

The magnitude of national-level differences in the timing and outcome of leaving home transitions has stimulated researchers to develop macro-level explanatory models. Quantitative analysis lends it itself to explanatory models that assume a rational, or quasi-rational, model of behaviour, where young people make decisions to leave home based on the range of opportunities and options available to them. In modelling transitions most attention has focused on the impact of education, labour market and socio-economic background (Corijn and Klijing, 2001), although more recently the impact of differential social assistance programmes has also emerged as a key explanatory factor of differences in the timing of transitions (Jurado Guerrero, 2001; Aassve et al., 2002). In particular, in explaining the distinctive 'southern' European pattern of late leaving, a range of socio-economic factors have been identified under which late leaving emerges as an economically rational decision. These factors are: characteristics of the southern European youth labour market and education system, specifically high rates of youth unemployment and insecure job opportunities coupled with a tradition for extended education and/or training; shortage of affordable housing and limited availability of rented accommodation; and finally, the lack of social assistance for young people, with a strong reliance on the family as *the* main provider of welfare for young people (Esping-Andersen, 1999; Jurado Guerrero, 2001; Baizán et al., 2002). The distinctive 'southern' pattern of leaving home is therefore clearly associated with structural factors that impinge on young people's lives, and is not just treated as a peculiarity of family life. Cultural explanations also have some validity here, as most analysts accede to the observation of the specificity of southern European family forms that emphasize the importance of family solidarity

(Reher, 1998). The problem for quantitative analysis is that it is difficult to measure these cultural differences, while labour market, education and social welfare characteristics are more readily quantifiable.

Education

Education has a complex relationship with leaving home and is very much a factor that varies between different contexts. What is important here is how the higher education system is organized. We can identify two broad approaches to the organization, delivery and funding of higher education, either a North American/north European model or a continental European approach (Roberts, 2004). In the latter young people spend a long time in education (university degrees may last for 5 or even 7 years), they are often more vocational in focus (the link with labour market transitions is more transparent) and, crucially for our study, often assume that young people live at home for the duration of their studies. Hence in this context transitions to higher education are compatible with delay in leaving home (for example for Spain, see Holdsworth, 2000). In contrast the North American/north European model is based on shorter periods of time in education, a more general approach to course of study (less emphasis on vocational courses with more students studying arts, humanities and social sciences) and a greater expectation that students will leave home, or at least live away from home, for the duration of their studies. The functional relationship between leaving home and going to university is quite distinct in the two models, although in practice individual experiences might vary, for example the continental model often allows for weekday students, who return home at weekends, while the North American model often assumes that students return home at vacation. In both cases these experiences do not involve a 'complete' departure from the parental home, but more of a half-way house, of 'living away' (Leonard, 1980) or 'semi-autonomy' (Goldscheider and DaVanzo, 1989).

Differences in the funding of education are also relevant, particularly the extent to which the cost of higher education is met by the state. From an English perspective student funding is very pertinent, as the structure of funding is currently being radically overhauled. The removal of maintenance grants and introduction of fees and loans have increased the costs of higher education and are associated, to a certain extent, with more young people living at home for the duration of their studies (Holdsworth and Patiniotis, 2004). However it is too simple to claim that where the state makes a greater contribution to education, young people are more likely to leave home. For example in the US there is a strong tradition of leaving home for education, despite the high personal costs that this might entail, although not surprisingly there is a strong class effect on leaving home to study (Goldscheider and DaVanzo, 1989).

However, the relationship between education and leaving home is not just a functional one that is determined by the arrangement of the university system. Going to university is more than just a case of acquiring qualifications, but, as Bourdieu contends, is also part of the process through which individuals build up their 'cultural capital' and through which social inequalities are perpetuated (Bourdieu and Passeron, 1977). Young people who have gone to university might have very different aspirations associated with different cultural capital, and are often more likely to emphasize their own autonomy. Hence another outcome of education transitions on leaving home is that the better educated are more likely to leave home prior to marriage, and this relationship is found in very different contexts, regardless of the underlying trend (Holdsworth, 2000).

(Un)employment

Leaving home is closely bound up with achieving, or as a marker of, economic independence. Throughout this book we interrogate the interrelations between leaving home and independence but, while we might accept that there is no simple relationship, we recognize at the very least that leaving home does involve a financial outlay and is much harder for young people with limited economic resources. Here, though, we are concerned not so much with how this relationship works out at an individual level, but at an aggregate one. The fact that there has been a near-universal trend towards delayed leaving home in modern industrial countries, despite the overall cross-national differences in timings, and that this has been concomitant with the collapse of the youth labour market, would appear to suggest that economic factors have played an important part in shaping leaving-home transitions in recent years. Iacovou and Berthoud (2001) suggest that unemployment should be treated as a stage in youth transitions, with over a quarter (28 per cent) of young people in Europe reporting a spell of unemployment prior to their careers. Even for those who secure employment, the probability of this being an insecure contract is high (over half of 17- to 20-year-olds).

However the relationship between labour market characteristics and leaving home is not always that transparent, and, as Aassve et al. (2002) summarize, the empirical literature on leaving home and economic variables give varying results. The impact that unemployment, or casual employment, has on leaving home transitions will very much depend on contextual factors. First at an individual level, being unemployed in a region of high unemployment might be very different to being out of work in a relatively buoyant labour market. In the former situation unemployment might expedite leaving home as young people leave to look for work elsewhere. Holdsworth et al.'s (2002) regional analysis of Spanish leaving-home transitions suggests this to be the case, as young people in southern Spain, where unemployment is higher, are more likely to leave than their counterparts in more prosperous areas. A second important consideration is gender, as Aassve et al. (2002: 269) demonstrate for southern Europe, women who are out of the labour force have a much higher rate of leaving home than their male counterparts.

A further important mediating factor is access to and level of social assistance that young people may receive. Aassve et al.'s (2002) analysis of the ECHP demonstrates that young people's earnings and employment have a stronger impact on the likelihood of leaving in southern Europe, compared with continental Europe, where earnings are less important. In Scandinavian countries, neither employment status or earnings impact significantly on leaving home transitions. This, they suggest, is indicative of the weaker role of the welfare state in the south, where young people have to rely either on their own earnings or their parents and there is no support from the state to either top this up or provide a substitute income. Hence young people's leaving-home transitions are more sensitive to labour market fluctuations in the south than elsewhere in Europe.

Social class

Young people's socio-economic backgrounds are closely related to their employment situation. While the association between class and outcomes may be more transparent for transitions in employment or education, when it comes to leaving home the causality is less obvious. This is in part, as Avery et al. (1992) argue, because it is possible to theorize two contradictory relationships between socio-economic background and propensity to leave home, which very much depend on the context of leaving. If, on the one hand, parents and adult children favour close contact and the maintenance of accepted standards of living, then young people from more privileged backgrounds may be more likely to delay leaving. If, however, privacy and independence are favoured then we would expect the opposite relationship. Moreover, we might find that the propensity for close contact or independence is in itself related to class position. Holdsworth's (2000) analysis of Spanish transitions suggests that while, on the whole, Spanish families favoured close contact and delayed leaving, there is evidence of accelerated leaving among more advantaged social classes.

Another perspective on the relationship between leaving home and social class is that young people from less advantaged backgrounds have access to fewer resources in the parental home and leave home at younger ages. Berrington and Murphy (1994) describe a U-shaped relationship between leaving home and class in Great Britain, as young people from the most and least privileged backgrounds leave at younger ages, the former usually for higher education, while we might speculate that the latter leave as they have no reason to stay, or their parents cannot afford to support them (Jones and Martin, 2003). However, Berrington and Murphy also suggest that this U-shaped relationship is partly determined by the economic situation, and that the propensity for less advantaged young people to leave earlier diminished during the 1980s.

Cross-national comparisons of the relationship between socio-economic background and the timing of leaving home illustrate that class does not necessarily speed up or delay transitions but the precise nature of the relationship depends on the context in which leaving home occurs and the range of opportunities that young people have available to them. Class advantage is not just made manifest through the transfer of material resources (such as parents financing young people's housing moves) but can also be reproduced through the transfer of non-material resources (De Jong Gierveld et al., 1991), that is cultural capital that enables some young people to more successfully negotiate some transitions, such as leaving home to go to university.

Housing

When young people leave home they need to find somewhere to live, so availability of suitable housing will impact on decisions to leave or not. Yet what actually constitutes suitable housing varies between different contexts. In the UK for example there is a clearly recognized 'youth' housing market, characterized by cheap and transitional housing mainly based in the private and social rented sector. This market, though, is being increasingly squeezed, reflecting both declining economic fortunes of young people as well as increased housing costs and expansion of the owner-occupied market (Ford et al., 2002). Both of these factors have stimulated much debate about the 'transitional' nature of youth housing and impact on transitions to adulthood in the UK (Ford et al., 2002; Heath and Cleaver, 2003). This pattern of squeezing out the private sector has been replicated elsewhere in northern Europe (Mulder and Wagner, 1998). However in countries such as Spain there is very little demand or supply for 'youth housing' as the ideal is for young people to buy a house on leaving home (Holdsworth and Irazoqui Solda, 2002). Hence the lack of available cheap accommodation in countries such as Spain is a factor influencing older leaving ages, but we might also speculate that even if this type of accommodation is available young people might not necessarily choose it.

Family structure

A final consideration that has emerged in North American/north European studies is the impact of family structure on leaving home. There is a consistent finding that parental divorce tends to expedite the process of leaving. In fact 'early leaving' is identified as one of the deleterious outcomes of divorce on children (Kiernan, 1992; Mitchell et al., 1989; Kiernan, 1992; Murphy and Wang, 1998). This trend is most discernible for girls and is also associated with other early transitions, such as out of education and into parenthood. Even in countries with much lower rates of divorce, the association between parental separation and early leaving holds (Holdsworth, 2000).

Aquilino (1991) attempted to provide further specification of the relationship between family structure and leaving home by considering a range of 'nonintact' family structures within the US. His general conclusion was that 'childhood family structure has a substantial impact on both the timing of first home-leaving and the pathway out of the parental home'. Adoption and non-parental living arrangements have the strongest effects and the effects are generally stronger for women than for men. Stable single-parent families from birth did not differ from intact families and children from non-intact families are more likely to move straight into independent households. His findings broadly were in line with other North American and North European studies.

Summary

The increasing availability of longitudinal data has facilitated quantitative analysis of leaving home transitions, which have been able to shed more light on the timing, outcome, relationship with other transitions and possible causal factors. As such the overall picture that emerges from this analytical approach is of the continuing importance of structures, particularly class divisions, on young people's destinations (Breen and Goldthorpe, 2001; Bynner et al., 2003; Roberts, 2003). Trying to pick out a consistent theme in these analysis is quite tricky, however, as one characteristic that emerges very strongly is the importance of local context. Even the most straightforward factors, such as economic variables, which we might expect to have a consistent impact on leaving home, will vary between different contexts. However, the most important overall trend is that towards delayed leaving, or at least more young people living with parents at older ages (in some cases these might be early leavers who have returned home). This observation hints at the importance of economic considerations, including housing, but also of the importance of family and parents (Molgat, 2002) who support these 'extended' transitions.

2 Methodological issues and theoretical approaches

In this chapter we shall explore some of the key methodological issues and theoretical orientations linked to the study of leaving-home transitions. We start by looking at the idea of 'transitions', considering the range of meanings attached to the term and the various ways in which these might be analysed. Next we consider ways of conceptualizing and analysing the contexts within which these transitions occur. The discussion of 'transition' and 'context' in this chapter reviews the main theoretical issues that are discussed in the theme-based chapters (Chapters 3 to 7). The chapter continues with a brief examination of a particular study conducted by the authors and concludes with some more general issues.

In this chapter we do not attempt to cover all the possible methodologies or social theories, nor do we present just one perspective, as we have found that the different aspects of leaving home raise distinctive theoretical issues and we have drawn influence from a range of theorists. Rather, we focus on those methodologies and theories that would seem to be most relevant to the topic under discussion and that have, in fact, sometimes been used in studies that have already been published. In the theme-based chapters that follow we develop specific theoretical perspectives that we have used to make sense of our different themes. Finally, we make no clear distinction between methodologies and theories, understanding theory to be already implied in the selection and discussion of methodologies.

Transitions

Individuals experience all kinds of transitions within their lives: beginning school, changing school, leaving school, getting married, becoming parents, getting divorced, beginning and leaving employment, and so on. The list, if not endless, is potentially very large. But of these, only a few are given particular or more general significance. Some of these will be the focus of ceremonies involving networks of individuals beyond the individuals concerned. And others, even where such ritual celebration does not normally take place, are frequently seen as important turning points in an individual's life. Leaving the parental home is one such transition.

Significant transitions take place within a life-course; indeed, it can be said that life-courses are organized around transitions. The idea of the life-course has been one of the most durable and influential concepts within the social sciences. It has proved to be a useful bridge between different disciplines – history, sociology, demography and so forth – and has provided useful theoretical and methodological links between the individual and society. It has often been seen as a practical realization of C. Wright Mills 'sociological imagination' (Mills, 1959), the linking of biography and history. The notion of a 'life-course' suggests a movement through time. Such a movement, or set of related movements, consists of three broad elements: an individual biography, a changing household context and processes of historical change. The life-course is concerned with the linking of these elements or, as Elder puts it, with the bond between age and time (Elder, 1978).

Use of the life-course idea does not necessarily imply a unified set of progressions within society. Whether or not life-courses, and the transitions around which they are organized, are more or less standardized is a matter for empirical investigation into particular historical circumstances (Anderson, 1985). There is a distinction, therefore, between the concept of the 'life-course', where diversity is possible, and both older notions of the 'life-cycle' and social-psychological accounts of the stages of human development.

While life-course has proved to be an enduring and useful concept in social science research, the concept of transition has come under considerable scrutiny in recent years (Cohen and Ainley, 2000; Bynner, 2001; EGRIS, 2001; MacDonald et al., 2001; Skelton, 2002; Valentine, 2003; Te Riele, 2004). This has been brought about due to empirical observations of the increasing fragmentary nature of youth transitions (Allatt, 1997) and theoretical developments that have identified the significance of the decline of traditional scripts and the rise of 'self-negotiated' biographies (Beck and Beck-Gernsheim, 2002; Cieslik and Pollock, 2002). As transitions become less bounded by established patterns, particularly around the time of leaving education and entering the labour market, young people have more opportunities to write their own scripts, but also face increasing risks of becoming marginalized (see, for example, Furlong and Cartmel, 1997; Valentine, 2003). The transition approach is also called into question from the tradition of youth cultural studies in that it focuses too much on the achievements (or more commonly the failings) of youth, and essentially how young people become adults, rather than the actuality of youth experiences. As Miles argues, the transition approach is dominated by a tendency to 'treat young people as troubled victims of economic and social restructuring without enough recourse to the active ways in which young people negotiate such circumstances in the course of their everyday lives' (Miles, 2000: 10). In assessing the contribution of the transition approach we echo MacDonald et al.'s (2001) view that the study of transitions does not necessarily have to fit Miles description, as transitions are not necessarily restricted to economic criteria, nor do they have to ignore young people's agency. However, at the very least we need to think through what we mean by the idea of 'transition'.

The idea of a transition in the sense being developed here does imply several things. Such transitions are part of the experiences of a significant proportion of the population, often, although not always, within a relatively narrow span of years; they are a matter of concern to individuals and institutions other than those most immediately involved and they are understood to be events of some significance even if they are not always marked by specific ceremonies. Another way of thinking about these transitions is that they can usually be anticipated in advance of the actual event. At some stage in the future one's son or daughter is expected to leave the parental home and to form some independent household and the same sense of future anticipation can be applied to various other life-course transitions. Similarly, leaving home is a matter of concern to a set of individuals outside those directly involved and is usually seen, in anticipation or in retrospect, as an event of some importance.

Although the idea of a transition does imply a movement from stage A to stage B, such transitions are not necessarily compressed or 'one-off' events. Very frequently they may consist of a series of events: 'I propose instead to describe transitions as long-term *processes* that result in a qualitative re-organization of both inner life and external behaviour' (Cowan, 1991: 5, his emphasis).

Even dramatic events such as a sudden death might be followed by a long period of adjustment and re-organization. In the case of leaving home this is usually anticipated, frequently planned for and takes place over a period that might be quite extended and that could include one or more returns to the parental home or other moves. As outlined in Chapter 2, the question 'when did you leave home?' is probably becoming more and more difficult to answer.

Transitions are the subject of moral evaluations, which is another way of saying that they are seen as events of some importance. These evaluations might apply to the transitions themselves distinguishing, say, between marriage and divorce or between births within or outside stable, heterosexual couple relationships. Or some sense of what is appropriate or inappropriate might apply to the timing of the transitions. Thus people may have a sense of the 'right' time to leave home, to marry, to start a family and so on. This is not to say that there is always complete uniformity or consensus in such ideas and, indeed, a key argument is the extent to which there has developed a greater sense of fluidity in these transitions (Hockey and James, 2003).

Writing more generally of the life-course, Jonsson (2001) considers the life-course under conditions of 'post-Fordism', noting a greater sense of unpredictability and some evidence of convergence between the trajectories of men and women. However, he argues that there is still not complete flux in family or other transitions and that there is sufficient predictability to justify the continuing use of the term 'life-course'. Put another way, in the context of our particular interests there still seems to be some sense of the 'right' time to leave home despite the fact that there may be some variability in this and that the leaving-home process itself might be extended over several months or years.

If we treat the idea of the transition out of the parental home (and all the other transitions that may or may not be associated with such a move) as a process over a period of time then we suggest that this period or process is itself of interest, apart from the stages that might be identified either side of this transition. (In this case these might be living in the parental home and living apart from the parental home.) A term that is sometimes used here to describe such periods is 'liminal' and the period is characterized as one of 'liminality'. This term has a variety of usages particularly within social anthropology and psychology. Very generally, the term can refer to a particular stage in life that is characterized as 'betwixt and between' or to the experiences of individuals located within this stage. Such a sense of liminality need not always be associated with unpleasant or painful experiences. It may sometimes be associated with a freedom from constraints or strong structured normative expectations. Examples here may be holidays or periods of travel abroad.

In the present case the term could refer to an uncertain location within a variety of oppositions, such as those between child and adult, dependence and independence, irresponsibility and responsibility and between the parental home and one's own home. As has already been suggested these oppositions do not always neatly map on to each other and, partly as a consequence of this, a sense of liminality around this time of life might be greater now than in earlier times. Thus there are the concerns with the experiences of the 'thresholders' (Apter, 2001) or with extended adolescence or delayed adulthood. Young people, it is argued, spend longer in this liminal or marginal state and the complexities associated with this state are all the greater. Much of this book will be devoted to exploring these complexities.

'Liminality' may also be linked to another important characteristic of inter-generational relations, which is ambivalence (Luescher and Pillemer, 1998). Sociologically, ambivalence is taken to occur where is there is a contradiction in norms and values (Merton and Barber, 1963), and we can usefully view one characteristic of liminality as being torn between practices and moral evaluations. Parents might want to help out their adult children but hold back in fear of spoiling or at least compromising their children's sense of achievement and independence. Alternatively, young people might eschew parental support in order to 'stand on their own two feet'.

While the use of the term 'liminality' does usefully point to a set of link-ages between structural conditions and lived experiences and thus can alert the researcher to some interesting issues, this usage does have some limita-tions. Firstly, the identification of the conditions for liminality does not neces-sarily mean that the individuals thus located will experience or understand it in this way. Second, the use of the term 'liminal' can (although this does not seem to be implied in the original usages) suggest that the stage is of some lesser significance than the stages on either side of this location (childhood and adulthood, for example)which are assumed to have a greater solidarity and reality. Against this one can argue that the stage of 'liminality' (if one wishes to characterize it this way) has its own reality and set of structured meanings. Further, the stages on either side are not in themselves more solid or more fixed than this transitional stage. Quite when childhood, adolescence and adulthood begin and what is entailed in these states are themselves matters of some complexity, which have been much discussed.

Linked to the idea of transitions within the life-course is the idea of 'gen-erations'. This has proved to be an elusive but fruitful idea in the history of sociological analysis (Edmunds and Turner, 2002). Generations may refer to sets of people born within a particular period of time, such as a decade (cohorts), to families, or in historically significant periods of time. Thus we might refer to individuals in England and Wales who were born in between 1950 and 1959, to our parents' or grandparents' generations or to looser characterizations such as the 'baby boomers', 'Thatcher's children' and so on.

Generations are linked to transitions in two ways. The first is that the persons undergoing the transitions are constituted as a future generation or a generation in the process of 'becoming'. This is probably another reason why this transition is seen as a matter of some importance. Here the generation might refer to a cohort within a particular nation or to something more strongly linked to family values and family continuity. Thus Rossi and Rossi (1990: 458) write: 'Each generation, then, carries its personal family history forward in time, and our understanding of the relationship between them is enriched by the knowledge of their shared past.' Transitions, therefore, are not just an individual story but also a family and an inter-generational story.

Another way of linking generation and transition is in terms of the kinds of comparisons that are made between leaving home 'then' and 'now'. The reference here may be to constructed and contrasting historical periods or to periods that are more clearly linked to familial generations. Thus the contrast may be between leaving home today and in our parents' (or grandparents') generation and the extent and ways in which it was easier or more difficult then than now. These may be actual generations linked to particular families or more generalized generations. An illustration of the latter is in Terri Apter's discussion of 'thresholders' (Apter, 2001: 176). Her point of reference is the current generation of young people who have left home or who are contemplating leaving home. For their grandparents' generation, she argues, entry into adulthood was at the age of 16 when they left school and found their first job. For their parents' generation it was after graduation. Today matters are much less clear cut and there is greater ambiguity about when an individual actually attains adulthood. Clearly, this characterization is greatly over-simplified and smoothes over a lot of variation in terms of class, gender and other distinctions. This illustration is chosen less for its accuracy and more as an example of the way in which the idea of generation may be used to provide a framework for describing social change.

Alongside the idea of generation or cohort we can also refer to the idea of 'the convoy'. This is a more recent idea (Kahn and Antonucci, 1980; Antonucci and Akiyama, 1995) but one which, in common with some of the other terms in this section, seeks to convey a sense of sets of people moving through time. They start out at more-or-less the same time, the point of departure being something like leaving school or graduation, and they move forward, being exposed to a least some common or similar experiences and living under similar historical circumstances. More recently, the idea of a convoy has been linked to the study of friendship over time (Pahl, 2000), although this idea does not necessarily require that each individual be in frequent contact with other 'members' of the same convoy. Individuals may leave a particular convoy and join up with others or may rejoin a convoy after a gap of some years. The idea of a convoy does appear to reflect the ways in which some people, at least, understand their experiences over time and illustrations of this way of conceptualizing the passage of time will be provided later in this book.

We have, therefore, a set of linked ideas including transitions, life-course, generations and cohorts. It can be seen that there are links and affinities between these ideas and that, in particular, what links them is a concern with time. Time has developed into a major concern within the social sciences and is now the subject of several important books and journals (Adam, 1990, 1995). We shall not attempt to explore these theoretical concerns in any detail. We stress, however, the importance of understanding different 'times' (personal time, family time, historical time and so on) and the idea of time as a resource around which there may be negotiation. For example, much of the negotiation that takes place within the parental home prior to the departure of a young person is frequently about issues to do with time keeping and being in the right place at the right time. Time spent in bed frequently becomes a core signifier of differential generational ideas of the use of time (Allatt and Yeandle, 1992). Alternatively, part of the attraction of leaving home and having a 'place of one's own' is also of having 'time of one's own' and being able to come and go as one pleases. We also see here the importance of understanding the linkages between time and space, a theme that, in different ways, runs through this book.

Transitions, therefore, take place within time and are themselves the subject of negotiation. This emphasizes the fact that in dealing with transitions we are dealing with, at least, two different levels. There is the more macro or historical level where we are concerned with regularities or changes in the overall patterning of transitions within a particular society or some other collectivity. In considering these regularities and changes we are concerned with matters such as structures and structuring and the role of normative definitions. On the other hand, there are the more micro transitions, relating more to individuals or particular families or households. Here concerns are more with experiences, negotiations and meanings. The relationship between these levels (part of the familiar tension between agency and structure that we discuss later on in this chapter) is a core theme within this book. For example, the meanings attached to 'home' and the process of leaving home are both generalized and particularized, both public and private.

We also need to locate transitions within a spatial context. If we think about the language that we use to describe youth transitions, very often this uses spatial metaphors such as pathways, trajectories and navigations. These metaphors, as Evans and Furlong (1997: 17) point out, 'have evolved in ways which reflect the dominant theoretical perspective of the time' from functionalism (pathways), through structuralist influences (trajectories), to reflexive approaches (navigations). Yet the ways in which these metaphors also imply spatial practices have received less attention (Valentine, 2003). Place tends to be invoked as part of the context of young people's lives, especially in case studies that depict how localized contextual effects impact on young people's experience (MacDonald and Marsh, 2001). Yet there is less focus on the spatial relations relating to young people's lives. In contrast to approaches to the significance of place, it is not necessarily appropriate to restrict our consideration of space to something that is given, but rather that as Lefebvre (1991: 82–3) contends: 'any space implies, contains and dissimulates social relationships – and this despite the fact that space is not a thing but rather a set of relations between things . . .'

A focus on how space is produced through practices has enriched our understanding of aspects of domestic routine (see, for example, Sibley, 1995; Valentine, 1999) and family relationships, particularly children, but the significance of space in young people's lives remains at the margins of youth research, particularly accounts of leaving home. Yet of all the components of youth transitions, leaving home is the one that is arguably most about space; it is it about taking responsibility, both economically and practically, for a new dwelling. Moreover it is about asserting a spatial independence from the family home, which underlies autonomy from parents. In fact the psychological aspects that link use of space and independence are just as important, if not more so. The desire for one's own space is an often heard lament in modern industrialized societies, and the advantages that having a room or place of one's own that this entails, of being in control and establishing physical and psychological distances from others, are clearly recognized. Yet, returning to Lefebvre, it is not sufficient to acknowledge that space matters, but that the production of space, which is so much part of leaving home, is as much about social relations as it is about more practical matters. The theme of spatial practices is recurrent throughout the book, particularly in the chapter on home, in which we draw further on Lefebvre to explore the relationship between meanings of home and leaving home.

Context

It has been suggested, at various stages in the argument, that the leaving-home transition does not take place in a vacuum but is influenced by the wider context in which it takes place. This is scarcely a novel or exceptional point of departure (Bynner et al., 1997). Irwin is only one among several researchers who seeks to look beyond the particularities of the life-course and to see it 'as an integral aspect of more general social arrangements' (Irwin, 1995: 1). More specifically, she is concerned with the ways in which the transition to adulthood has changed over time and the ways in which these changes may be related to changes in the 'gender- and age-related patterning of rewards to employment' (Irwin, 1995: 93). She is also concerned with changes in household structure.

Irwin's argument has much in common with other researchers in this and other related fields, although there are differences in emphasis between her account and these other studies. But what do we mean by 'context' and what does it mean to seek to place leaving home transitions in relation to some wider context? In the first place we can argue that there is no such thing as a context-free transition. Transitions are not part of some biologically driven set of inevitabilities but vary within and between societies and cultures and over time. This is despite the fact that biological analogies, such as references to birds leaving the nest, are often used. At a very abstract level we may say that the context is part of the social environment within which transitions take place and within which these transitions are included. The context is, therefore, to some extent something that is external to any particular transition but that is assumed to have some kind of influence over this transition. Very broadly, and equally abstractly, we can distinguish four different, although not exclusive, ways of characterizing this context

Wider social institutions

In the first place we may consider those institutions or sets of institutions within which the participants in a transition are included and that, to this extent, overlap with these transitions. Most of the literature has given considerable emphasis to the economy, in particular the changing structuring of the labour market as it affects young people (Hutson and Jenkins, 1989; Allatt and Yeandle, 1992; Jones and Wallace, 1992; Irwin, 1995; Jones, 1995). The structuring of the labour market and patterns of youth unemployment are seen as delaying the time of departure from the parental home and of elongating or making less clear-cut the overall period of transition (Molgat, 2002). As outlined in Chapter 1, other institutional factors that are frequently seen as significant include changes in education, especially the expansion of higher and further education, and changes in family and household structure. The structuring of the housing market is also seen as being of crucial importance, especially since the 1980s (Ford et al., 2002).

Social characteristics

Another rather similar way of understanding the context is in terms of social characteristics that are part of the identities of the people involved in the transitions. Here we are recognizing that we are not simply dealing with 'young people' but with young people who are united or divided by numerous other social characteristics such as gender, social class and ethnicity. These other aspects of social structure have their own dynamics and are found to be influential in various other areas of social life as well as life-course transitions.

Broad historical trends

The context may also be defined in terms of broad historical trends or currents that are seen as influencing a wide range of societies. One particular example of this is the notion of globalization. While, in the current work, we do not lay a great deal of emphasis upon this highly influential idea, it can be argued that globalization makes its impact upon the transition to adulthood in a variety of ways. For one thing, many of the economic trends that are seen as having an impact on the transition (casual or short-term employment, flexibilization and so forth) may themselves be linked to more global trends (McDowell, 2003). Global transformations in gender relations have also been seen as having an impact on households and family relations (Castells, 1997), which, in their turn are sometimes seen as affecting life-course transitions. Further, global notions of youth and youth culture, mediated through increasingly globalized communications media, are sometimes seen as contributing to the delayed entry into adulthood. At present, however, the notion of globalization seems to be a little difficult to operationalize partly because of the variety of ways in which the term is defined or understood. Consequently, its impact on particular life-course transitions is itself difficult to assess although it is likely that this might prove to be a fruitful area for enquiry in the future.

A more fruitful line of enquiry may be associated with the concept of individualization, associated especially with the work of Ulrich Beck and Elizabeth Beck-Gernsheim (1995, 2002). 'Individualization' is to be distinguished from ideas of 'individualism' although the terms are sometimes confused. The latter is associated with political or moral philosophy, broadly located within the classic traditions of liberal thought. Here the emphasis is upon the individual as a moral agent, exercising informed choices in a context broadly described as democratic. 'Individualization', in contrast, refers to a broad social process, arising out of changes in the economy and market relations together with changes in the organization of domestic life and the gender order. The outcome of these currents is a stress on a particular construction of the individual. Unlike the individual of liberal political and economic thought, this individual is, paradoxically, compelled to choose. It is necessary for this individual to construct his or her own biography out of the social resources and capitals that are available.

The relevance of individualization for the present discussion is that it raises the question as to how far it is the individuals' own responsibility to decide when and how to leave home. 'Traditional' prescriptions as to the right time or the right way to leave have decreasing influence. An individual might decide to remain in the parental home, to leave home and to set up an independent dwelling or to move in with a partner. Alternatively, she might have some transitional arrangements such as student accommodation or a period of travel abroad. A variety of trajectories are possible. The point would seem to be less one of what decisions are made and more one of the point of reference for or legitimation of such decisions. This point of reference would seem to be less in terms of normative expectations found within the wider community and more in terms of the individual herself. This is partly with reference to individual preferences and, more fundamentally, to notions of the individual self and personal identity. It might be argued that individualization is less to do with actual practices and more to do with the accounting procedures associated with these practices, in other words the moral basis upon which such practices are enacted.

There are numerous questions to be raised about the concept of individualization, not least the questions raised by the experiences of those whose transitions appear to be very much shaped by external forces over which they have little control. Other questions refer to the level of generalization, the extent to which the concept of individualization is held to apply to all 'modern' or 'late modern' societies, defining societies in terms of nation states. As illustrated in Chapter 1, quantitative studies reveal clear differences between countries in terms of the timing of leaving home as well as in relation to other family indicators. How far do such variations call into question more generalized or global notions such as individualization? And if such variations can be seen as significant how can researchers account for them?

Regimes and cultures

This leads us to a fourth way of understanding context, which refers less to global-type trends, assumed to be influential over a wide range of countries, and more to the distinct characteristics of particular nations or areas and how these differ from each other.

One framework for analysing differences has been provided by Esping-Andersen (1999) in his analysis of different welfare regimes. He has developed a framework for the analysis of different welfare regimes, comparing and contrasting, for example, the more public welfare societies associated with Nordic countries with the liberal regimes of the UK and the US and the familialistic regimes of countries such as Spain and Italy. To simplify the argument considerably, the different ways in which welfare (especially organized care for the more vulnerable members of society) can be arranged varies according to the different balance between the role played by each of three elements: the state, the market and the family. Each one of these elements has its part to play in modern societies although the mix and the emphasis will differ between societies. Within this kind of comparative framework we can begin to explore variations in terms of the structures of values and practices along such continua as individualistic/solidaristic and interventionist/non-interventionist. Such a framework for analysis might at least suggest that individualization (or globalization) is not the whole story and that the kinds of tendencies identified by Beck and others may be modified by state interventions or more traditionalistic or familalistic values.

Another way of characterizing differences between (and within) nations has been in terms of 'culture'. In trying to account for differences in youth transitions that are loosely defined by regional or national boundaries, or by social cleavages along class or ethnic divisions, it may sometimes seem appropriate to make sense of these distinct patterns with reference to cultural factors, rather than treating variation as essentially reducible to economic criteria. For example, differences in timing of leaving home cannot be explained simply by reference to levels of youth unemployment, available and affordable housing and social assistance but also with reference to culturally prescribed behaviour. However in moving beyond economic determinism, we have to recognize that it is not satisfactorily to replace it with determinism of a cultural type, where social actors are treated as little more than cultural dopes (Kertzer, 1997). As Hammel (1990) comments, the structural-functionalist approach to culture was rejected sometime ago by anthropologists, who have moved towards treating culture as a 'negotiated symbolic understanding', where 'culture is continuously created and reshaped in the course and by the process of social interaction' (Hammel, 1990: 465). Greenhalgh (1988, 1990) also argues that culture should be regarded as a process, which takes meaning in the way it is reproduced through individual behaviour. Moreover, culture is 'highly variable' and 'culture is like a spice racks of ideas and practices from which people choose depending on the menu of opportunities and constraints posed by their environments' (Greenhalgh, 1988: 668).

From this perspective culture is not approached as a series of abstract rules dictating individual behaviour, but as a collection of rules and practices (which Swidler, 1986, describes as a 'tool-kit') from which individuals select according to their own resources. This action approach to culture draws strongly on Geertz's interpretation of culture that 'men [sic] communicate, perpetuate, and develop their knowledge about and attitudes toward life' (Geertz, 1973: 89). Culture is not therefore reducible to values and norms (that people act in a certain way to achieve a certain objectives or outcomes) but culture is part of action itself and not distinguishable from it. In this way alternatives patterns of behaviour are recognized but tend be edited out as inappropriate in a particular cultural context. For example, young people in Spain do not leave home generally as teenagers because they regard this behaviour as inappropriate in a Spanish context, although they are aware that in other countries young people do leave home earlier.

One potential pitfall in treating culture in this way is that it can be treated as objectified rules or descriptors that are 'out there' and that people can pick and choose to suit their circumstances. In order to avoid this interpretation it is necessary to identify not just *how* young people's experiences differ but the processes through which young people negotiate with cultural practices and the meanings inscribed in individual transitions. The circular motion between culture and practice will serve to reinforce the legitimation of certain practices, particularly as young people will observe their peers making similar choices in similar situations, which reinforces the sense of 'it is what we do here'.

When considering leaving home the most important cultural indicator is the age at which young people leave. This suggests that young people respond to prescriptive age norms that define the lower age limit at which a young person is too young to leave and an upper age limit by which a young person should have left home (Settersten, 1998; Billari and Micheli, 2001). These age limits may vary across social and cultural contexts, as outlined in Chapter 1, but also allow for individuals to adapt them to their own circumstances (the fact that young people may recognize an age by which they *should* leave home, does not necessarily mean that they will leave home by that age). However there is a danger here in that stressing the importance of age norms makes them appear as little more than abstract rules. Nor, as Marini (1984) argues, do age norms tell us anything about the social, economic and cultural origins of differences in the timing of life-course events.

The danger of over-abstraction of cultural practices is highlighted in research at later stages of the life-course. In her influential study of family responsibilities, Finch (1989) argues that these are not defined by abstract rules but that understandings of 'the proper thing to do' emerge over time and in specific contexts, reflecting both individual circumstances as well as social and cultural contexts. We may expect the same processes for leaving home, with young people and their parents continually redefining expectations of leaving the parental home, with respect to both age norms and legitimated practices (for example leaving home to go to university, to marry, and to find a job) and individual circumstances. Leaving and returning to the parental home may also modify expectations of residential autonomy. Moreover it is difficult to separate expectations of the timing of leaving home from motivations to leave. For example leaving home at a young age to go to university may be more 'acceptable' and more common than leaving home at the same age to get married.

Cultural practices regarding leaving home will not just be restricted to timing but will incorporate expectations of parental obligation to support adult children either in the home, or during the transition. The importance of the family group has been incorporated into analysis of leaving home, as the increased availability of longitudinal survey data facilitates the inclusion of information on family background into models of leaving home (Mitchell et al., 1989; Aquilino, 1990; De Jong-Gierveld et al., 1991; Whittington and Peters, 1996). Yet the interpretation of these models has mostly concentrated on how the family may influence the financial implications of leaving home or staying put, although reference is also made to family structures. Hence familial influence is regarded as an extension of the economic basis for leaving home, and less attention has been given to expectations and limits to parental support reflecting culturally defined familial obligations (see, though, Goldscheider et al., 2001; Jones and Martin, 2003; Holdsworth, 2004). Yet the context of the family is more than just a group of individuals and the question of support and context is more than if parents make a financial contribution to young people. Rather, following Bourdieu, it is a collective subject directed towards accumulation and transmission of cultural and material resources. From this perspective the exchange of family resources at the time of leaving home, is not just treated as an economic utility but raises questions about the cultural expectations of parental support for adult children and how these are realized through inter-generational exchanges. This area has not been adequately addressed in studies of leaving home; we know relatively little about how parents' and children's expectations of parental responsibility vary across time and place. Our approach, which we develop in Chapter 7, uses Bourdieu's theory of practice and habitus to explore the embedded experiences of leaving home.

Yet the mediation of context does not just take place at an individual or familial level. In thinking through the various ways in which individuals assimilate context, we have found it useful to evoke Mead's concept of the generalized other. Mead (1934: 154) takes the generalized other to refer to the community to which an individual belongs. For Mead it is not sufficient for an individual to recognize the attitudes of others towards herself – she also needs to take on board 'their attitudes toward the various phases or aspects of the common social activity or set of social undertakings in which, as members of an organized society or social group, they are all engaged' (Mead, 1934: 155). Thus the ways in which young people might talk about what 'other people might expect' or 'other people do', are often tools by which people think through how they see others' actions and beliefs, but also how other people respond to them.

We have considered a variety of ways in which the context within which transitions to adulthood might be conceptualized. To recap, we can see the context as:

- institutions or sets of practices that affect this particular transition; in particular, the labour market, the housing market, education and the state;
- social characteristics that unite and divide individuals involved in the transition to adulthood; chiefly, gender, class and ethnicity;
- broad historical trends that are thought to have an impact upon life-course transitions in a whole range of late-modern societies; two main candidates here are globalization and individualization;
- more specific ways in which societies may be distinguished from each other; here we focus on welfare regimes and cultural differences.

Very broadly it can be seen that these different ways of understanding the context either overlap with or include, within some wider framework, the transitions to adulthood.

Studying transitions

One of the main rationales for studying young people's lives is to unpack the processes of transitions to adulthood; our interest in studying youth is often stimulated because it is a time of accentuated change (although in doing so we should not assume that youth is the only time of transitions in the life-course, nor that their transitions are linear and necessarily sequential). Focusing on youth as a 'process of becoming' (Allatt, 1997: 94) implicitly recognizes the importance of agency, that transitions are to a certain extent the outcome of individual choices and actions. In common with recent developments in the sociology of childhood (James and Prout, 1997; James et al., 1998), there is growing recognition of the need to place young people's (and children's) experiences at the heart of research on youth and childhood. As such, research methodologies in youth research need to give voice to young people's own experiences, while recognizing how young people are not completely free to write their own biographies. This generates a number of tensions in order to recognize both sides of young people's experiences; not only the definitive sociological dualism between structure and agency but also the need to develop research strategies that are sensitive to the potential conflict between the approaches of auto/biography and the ways in which transitions are categorized. That is, in order to make sense of how structural factors impinge on young people's biographies, we need to be able to compare young people from similar backgrounds, particularly looking at the relationships between class, gender, ethnicity and locality. As such we are often trying to situate young people into discrete social groups while acknowledging that their own biographies might be taking them on very individualized paths.

In recognizing the competing ways of interpreting young people's lives, it is relevant to consider a range of different methodologies that might be appropriate in unpacking the nuances and complexities of transitions. In particular, we can see how both quantitative and qualitative methods can be usefully applied to develop a more rounded understanding of young people's lives. Many youth studies fall on either side of the quantitative/ qualitative divide, but the applicability of mixed – methods to transitions research has also been recognized, particularly the combination of survey data to 'describe' dominate patterns and trajectories and qualitative data to flesh out more individual meanings. For example, the recent Economic and Social Research Council's research programme on youth citizenship and social change incorporated a number of projects that adopted a mixed methods approach to explore transitions relating to housing, employment, education and the inter-relationships between these. A common research design is to combine a quantitative survey to map out and describe the patterns and trajectories of young people's lives and to follow this up with more in-depth interviews exploring how these are realized by individual actors.

Though mixed methods are becoming increasingly popular, the quantitative/qualitative split is still very much discernible in youth research. Analysis of quantitative data has enriched our understanding of the complexity and variation in young people's lives. In particular, as reviewed in the previous chapter, the increased availability of longitudinal data, mainly in Europe and the US, has facilitated the analysis of youth transitions. The application of event history modelling techniques to this kind of longitudinal data is very appropriate for unpacking the structural factors that impinge on youth transitions, particularly regarding the timing and destination of transitions. However the time points at which transitional events happen have, by necessity, to be fixed so it is less clear how to deal with the processes inherent in these transitions. Hence it is harder to get a sense of the variability and individual complexity of youth transitions from quantitative models although this is by no means impossible. Moreover, these models are restrictive if we wish to be sensitive to variations in meanings, practices and understandings in individual accounts.

In order to elicit a more detailed understanding of meanings and negoti-ated practices of youth transitions, it is necessarily to adopt a qualitative approach. Biographies can be constructed retrospectively but the analysis of transitions lends itself to the more dynamic methods, through the collection of longitudinal qualitative data (Thomson and Holland, 2003). The collection of data over time allows for a more detailed understanding of the ways in which biographies are constructed and the contextual significance of young people's experiences and meanings. What matters to young people at one point in their lives in a particular location, such as taking part in activities while at university to build up social networks, might be less important in a different context. With the benefit of hindsight we can look back at our past experiences and provide a *post hoc* rationalization of why we acted in a particu-lar way, which might not appear as evident to us at the time, hence retro-spective biographies might generate a very different set of meanings associated with certain practices. However, while the collection and analysis of qualita-tive longitudinal data clearly has important advantages it is also costly in terms of time and money. One way of addressing the need for more dynamic biographies is through interviewing young people at different stages, includ-ing older generations, for example by collecting data both from young people and their parents.

In recent years the use of the narrative approach in social science research has become increasingly popular and we can talk about the emergence of a 'narrative turn'. A narrative approach can consider not just the stories that indi-viduals tell about their lives but why and how these stories are recounted. As Riessman (1993: 2) remarks, locating these narratives for analysis is not difficult as they are 'ubiquitous in everyday life'. Narratives form part of everyday con-versations but they can also take on deeper significance, particularly when used in psychotherapy, or in the current vogue for 'confessional' television pro-grammes where participants are encouraged to legitimate their narratives. Narratives are therefore a key way in which we make sense of our lives and can help to tie events together and understand the interconnections between events that might feel quite disparate at the time. As such a narrative frame-work lends itself particularly well to the study of transitions. Narrative accounts also offer different approaches for analysis, either within individual narratives (this can be particularly complex for longitudinal data – see Thomson and Holland, 2003) or across individuals, comparing events (such as leaving home) and accounting for structural differences (for example, class, gender, ethnicity, location).

Yet the narrative approach has weaknesses, particularly in that it can force the researcher into a particular way of thinking and interpreting data. One potential difficulty is the tendency to focus on what appear as more complete or full narrative accounts. When presenting data, detailed stories and lively accounts make for more interesting research papers. Yet it is often what people miss out from their accounts, either deliberately or because they have no experience of a particular event or meaning, that is most relevant. For example in our research on leaving home, young people who had a difficult time in the parental home, rather than talking at length about their experiences and negative emotions that they might equate with home, tended to have little say about what home meant to them, and identified themselves as being homeless. Their lack of a sense of home is what is significant here, although this is not necessarily clearly expressed. Hence in analysing data from a narrative perspective we need to be alert to the absences and the hesitancies and the questions that respondents find 'difficult' or maybe avoid answering. We also have to anticipate that not all people will provide narratives in the conventional sense and will use and construct time in different ways, often distinguishing between personal and historical time. Yet the way that time is used by respondents will depend on how the interviews are conducted. If respondents are invited to give a chronological account, this will provide a different perspective than if they are allowed to develop their own time frame. Further, narratives seem to function in different ways for different people, as illustrations of more general or more abstract points or as a form of presentation of self.

Finally, when interviewing young people it can often be difficult to build up the kind of rapport in an interview setting that will encourage respondents to 'open up' and talk at length and depth about their lives. In part this is socially determined: young people's views are treated as marginal, with authenticity and legitimacy of experiences associated with longevity. If young people are used to being told that their experiences 'don't count for anything' because they 'haven't really lived' then this might make it difficult for them to respond to an interviewer. We often find there is a gender imbalance here – many researchers who work with young people report particular problems in recruiting young men to take part in the research process. This might reflect how young men are marginalized from institutions or people in authority. For many young men a brush with authority will often mean that they been in trouble with the police whereas women are more likely to have come into contact with a wider range of social services, especially if they have children. The construction of individual narratives for young people is therefore, not without its problems.

Analysing transitions in context

The remaining question to consider here is how the relationship between a specific life-course transition and the context, however understood, might be analysed. In a very broad sense it might be assumed, from reading the available literature, that the relationship is a causal one moving from context to transition. More specifically, it is frequently argued that there have been significant changes in the process of leaving the parental home, broadly in the direction of a lengthening of the transition period and increasing uncertainty and ambiguity, and that these changes can be explained in terms of changes within these contextual factors (Evans and Furlong, 1997; Roberts, 1997). It should be stressed that these contextual factors, as outlined above, should not necessarily be seen as the source of competing explanations. Indeed, they are frequently combined. Thus an account that stresses the impact of changes in the labour market may see these changes in the context of more global processes and as mediated or shaped by both the social characteristics of the young people undergoing the transition and particular features of the culture within which it is taking place. For the individuals concerned it might seem that the apparently free choice of leaving home at a particular stage in one's life is in fact shaped, or even determined, by a whole host of 'external' factors to do with the economy, broad historical currents and particular cultural factors. In terms of the familiar contrast between 'agency' and 'structure', the emphasis would seem to be very much on the latter. Put very simply, the experience of a young person leaving home in Britain today is very different from the experiences of a similar individual in the 1950s or in the early part of the twentieth century and that these differences may be attributed to the range of contextual factors already indicated. There would, therefore, seem to be little scope for the exercise of individual initiative or choice. Even where, as in the case of discussions of individualization, choice would seem to be central, this individualism is itself shaped by other economic and social currents.

The various ways in which the tensions between individual agency and social structure (context, in our terms) might be resolved or transcended have constituted a core theme within sociological enquiry. The present set of issues dealing with life-course transitions constitute a particular illustration of this more general debate. Without claiming to resolve these issues, we are able to provide some pointers derived from the leaving-home literature and our own research.

A point of departure may be found in Raymond Williams' discussion of the complexities of the word 'determine' and, in particular, the contrast between a process which seems absolute and fixed and a process whereby certain limits are set (Williams, 1983: 98–102). Clearly, if we are thinking of some kind of causal relationship between context and transition this is one of determination only in the latter sense of the word. The stress within sociological analysis on probabilistic rather than absolute causal explanations also points in the same direction. On the other side, a whole host of similar words have been deployed to give some sense of individual agency. These include metaphorical terms such as 'strategy' and 'negotiation'. These terms have developed within sociological research in order to provide alternatives to accounts that seemed to give greater weight to external structural or normative pressures.

However, these terms themselves do not necessarily imply absolute freedom on the part of the individual agent. 'Strategies' (for example, housing
strategies – see Pickvance and Pickvance, 1995) refer to the deployment of
particular resources or capitals that are almost certainly unequally distributed
between individuals. Again, the parties to a process of negotiation are not
necessarily equal and have different kinds and amounts of resources at their
disposal. Further, the deployment of strategies and negotiations takes place
within a particular cultural context that 'determines' (in the broad sense of the
word) the limits within which such transactions may take place. All the existing studies of the leaving-home process give some version of this 'negotiation
within limits' model. Thus Jones and Wallace (1992) deploy a variety of oppositions such as process/structure, public/private and constraint/choice and
argue that the life-course approach provides a useful way of dealing with the
agency/structure divide (Jones and Wallace, 1992: 142). Jones' deployment of
the terms 'risks' and 'strategies' (Jones, 1995) points in the same direction.

In part, the question at issue here is one of levels of analysis. Statistical
analysis can point to broad trends and patterns, regularities that change over
time. Another way of thinking about structure is in terms of these regularities
and the institutions and norms that support them. At the more experiential
level, where qualitative research is more appropriate, the concern is with negotiations and strategies. The concern is also with meanings, those modes of
understanding and evaluating life-course transitions that are an integral part
of these transitions. But the processes of negotiation and sense making are
carried out in a context that is not random but has degrees of predictability
and order about it. Perhaps the task, at least in relation to the specific topics
examined in this book, is less one of providing some overall reconciliation
between agency and structure than to explore how these interact in particular
contexts and in relation to particular topics. Thus we might be concerned with
the idea of home and the way in which there appear to be quite similar understandings within, and in some cases at least, between countries. Or we may be
concerned with a topic such as adulthood where the range of variation in
understandings appears to be somewhat greater.

Use of comparative methods

To date, most comparative analyses of youth transitions have been based on
analysis of quantitative data and, as discussed in the previous chapter, have
provided detailed information on patterns and structural determinants of
young people's transitions in different contexts. Analyses of this type have
proved extremely useful in identifying the main contextual differences in
young people's lives and have sought to elucidate the structural factors associated with different patterns, particularly individual-level variables such as

class, gender and education and macro-economic factors such as level of youth unemployment, availability of housing and welfare support.

The main limitations of quantitative studies are how to measure and model those aspects of 'context' that cannot be easily measured in a standardized form. In particular trying to incorporate 'culture' can be problematic and measures of culture are often reduced to objective criteria that do not necessarily have much bearing on cultural differences, such as measures of religious attendance or normative attitudes towards family and personal lives. In this way culture is treated as another set of variables to be added to the right-hand side of a regression model (Kertzer, 1997). An alternative approach is to treat cultural values as those that cannot be measured. As such they are left to account for unexplained variation. 'Cultural' becomes a catch-all device for differences that cannot be measured by more objective criteria. Yet neither of these approaches come close to treating context, or culture, in the way we would wish to use it. We need therefore to develop methodologies that are sensitive to reflexive and embodied accounts of culture, and in doing so draw out the processes and practices through which young people negotiate with ideologies about home, independence and adulthood.

In order to move beyond an economic deterministic paradigm, but at the same time not to fall into the trap of cultural determinism, the most appropriate way to explore how young people negotiated with cultural practices is from the analysis of comparative qualitative data. There have been relatively few attempts to carry out comparative qualitative analysis of transitions and there are important methodological and practical issues that have contributed to this. On the practical side, organizing the collection of comparative data is intensive and time consuming. Yet the methodological problems are more serious. In undertaking comparative research we might want to seek out why and how young people act differently in different contexts. For example, why do young people leave home at older ages in southern Europe compared to northern Europe? Analysis of qualitative data will generate a rich interpretation of individual biographies in different contexts that are pertinent to unpacking *how* young people experience different transitions in varying contexts, yet it is more difficult to answer *why*. There is a methodological trap here, in that in order to provide an account of cultural differences, we have to collect individual accounts, and in doing so lose the benefits of being able to generalize about our findings. Of course this problem is not just specific to comparative analysis of youth studies (all social science research is, after all, at some level comparative, for example comparing young people from different class positions) yet it is at the core of the kinds of the problems we are considering here, because one of the main research questions we might be expected to provide an answer to is *why* do young people leave home later in Spain?

The solution is not straightforward. First, we can reject the question as too simplistic and one that cannot be answered in a straightforward way. This, however, is just avoiding the issue. Second, we can use qualitative data to explore a variety of different experiences and in doing so to try to match between different groups of young people: class background, family type (rather loosely lone-parent families or two-parent families), young people who leave home early or leave home late. The mix-and-match approach does not solve the problem of generalizing. It does, however, allow for more detailed analysis of the different strategies adopted in specific contexts, which might reveal either a dominant cultural model (everyone does the same regardless of background, and so forth) or more fragmented accounts.

It has to be recognized that all methodological approaches have their difficulties and the point is to provide some kind of match between the questions one wants to ask and the methodologies deployed. Thus, if we are interested in processes of negotiation and the strategies employed then some kind of qualitative approach is the most appropriate. We are, therefore, interested in how the transitions are negotiated, between whom and the ways in which these transitions are understood by the various parties involved. We wish to remain alert to complexities while going beyond an analysis that is simply a collection of individual accounts. We are therefore interested in hints, suggestions, tendencies and possibilities. In conducting the research we seek to enlarge our understanding of some of our key theoretical ideas – negotiation, strategy, 'generalized other' and so on – as well as the specific issues associated with leaving the parental home. Perhaps the question is less one of being able or not able to generalize but of the kind of generalization that we wish to make.

Our study

Our study was set up to explore young people's and their parents' experiences of leaving home and living together in three distinctive European contexts. The fieldwork was carried out in three European cities: Liverpool in the UK, Trondheim in Norway and Bilbao in Spain. These three countries were chosen because they are representative of very different leaving-home transitions as discussed in Chapter 1. With differences in timing (the youngest in Norway, followed by UK then Spain) and destinations (early leaving prior to marriage in Norway and UK, older leaving for marriage in Spain). We also chose these countries because, at least at a macro level, we can identify contextual factors relating to welfare regimes and family cultures. The three countries cover different approaches to welfare, from a universalistic regime in Norway (social democratic in Esping Andersen's typology) to a more market-based approach in the UK (equating to Esping Andersen's liberal type, though with vestiges of the universalistic provision) and a conservative regime in Spain that relies heavily on the family as the main provider of welfare (a familialistic regime). One of the most important aspects of the differential provision of welfare in the three countries for this study is the differing ways in which family support underlies that provided by the state. In focusing on these three countries we can, therefore, explore the ways in which families negotiate support in three very different welfare regimes. Thus our study looks at context in terms of the different culture and welfare regimes. It also considers context in terms of the different social groupings to which individuals might belong as well as the institutions (work and education, chiefly) that might affect their experiences.

Interviews were carried out with a mixture of young people and, if possible, their parents between May 2001 and September 2002 in and around each of the three cities. Most first contacts with the families involved were made with the young person, although this did not necessarily happen. Respondents were contacted using a modified snowballing technique, through a combination of friendship networks, youth organizations and institutions (for example, higher education institutions). Respondents were recruited to fulfil a quota based on gender/residential status (living at home/left) and employment status (employed/not working/student). Where possible we interviewed parents (in some cases just one parent, in others both) however we did not use willingness of parents to take part as a criterion for recruiting young people. In some cases this was not feasible either due to practical reasons (usually that young people no longer lived geographically close to their parents – in two cases parents and children did not live in the same country), or because the relationship between young people and parents had broken down and young people would not give their consent to us talking to their parents. This happened in all three countries. We also found, particularly in Liverpool, that some parents were reluctant to talk to us, even though their children were happy for us to do so. The most usual reason given was 'pressure of work/not enough time'. To obtain a less biased sample of parents we also interviewed a few parents in Liverpool and Trondheim independent of their children.

We attempted to recruit respondents from a range of different class backgrounds and have attempted to ascribe a class identity to all of the young people interviewed, although in doing so we recognize that the complexity of class for young people at a time of transition makes it quite hard to define. In particular, is a young person's class position determined by her parents, or her own position? For example Carlota comes from a poor farming family in rural Galicia, she left home when she was 12 to live with her sister and brother-in-law in order to carry on her studies and has since graduated as a lawyer, how then do we define her class 'background'? The answer is 'it depends', if we are looking at the experiences of a student, we might consider it more appropriate to take their parents' position, as they have not yet entered employment. Yet if we are examining the views of young people who have left home (or even are still living at home) who have finished education and started a career, then it is going against their actual experiences (and is potentially misleading) to identify their class position from that of their parents. This is a problem of young people in 'liminality', but also links to the importance of subjective under-standing of class rather than treating class position as an objective marker that can neatly be ascribed with reference to occupation and employment status (Skeggs, 1997).

Although our class indicators are quite crude (we simply distinguish between working and middle class), we have more working-class respondents in Liverpool, particularly among the women. This came about as we had the opportunity to recruit from a young person's housing project in Liverpool, although we did not come across similar enterprises in either Trondheim or Bilbao. The accounts of these women, particularly Sharon and Helen, stand out in contrast to others, as they clearly found the process very difficult at a young age. It is important to recognize the potency of their accounts but at the same time not to treat them as distinctive from the rest of the respondents.

The interviewees were divided between young people who had left and those living at home (27 young people were living at home, 31 had left or were temporarily living at home). Differences in the characteristics of respondents (particularly the slightly older age range in Bilbao) reflect the different patterns of leaving home in the three countries – for instance, as leaving home occurs at older ages in Bilbao, in interviewing around the process of leaving home we ended up with an older sample. The final breakdown of the sample is as follows:

Liverpool women at home: 6
Emma, Nina, Lynn, Rachel, Ally and Rebecca
Age range: 18–35
Linked with parents: 3
Class background: 3 middle class, 3 working class

Liverpool men at home: 5
Marc, Simon, Robert, Neil and Martin
Age range: 21–23
Linked with parents: 2
Class background: 2 middle class, 3 working class

Liverpool women away from home: 9
Catherine, Adele, Helen, Amber, Sharon, Sarah, Jane, Hannah, Lisa
Age range: 17–29
Linked with parents: 2
Class background: 3 middle class, 6 working class

Liverpool men away from home: 4
Matthew, Chris, Anthony and Gareth
Age range: 20–29
Linked with parents: 1
Class background: 2 middle class, 2 working class

Interviews with three additional Liverpool parents were carried out:

One lone mother living with all her children
One married father not living with children
One lone mother living with two of her children (two have left)

Trondheim women at home: 5
Kari, Hilde, Katrine, Marte and Yvonne
Age range: 19–28
Linked with parents: 3
Class background: 4 middle class, 1 working class

Trondheim men at home: 3
Kjell, Sian and Ben Obi
Age range: 25–26
Linked with parents: 0
Class background: 1 middle class, 2 working class

Trondheim women away from home: 4
Kristine, Anne Bente, Andrea and Siv
Age range: 21–27
Linked with parents: 2
Class background: 3 middle class, 1 working class

Trondheim men away from home: 4
Espen, Odd, Joar, Eivind
Age range: 25–28
Linked with parents: 0
Class background: 2 middle class, 2 working class

Interviews with three additional Trondheim parents were carried out:

One married mother living with one child and two step-children (one has left)
One married mother not living with children
One married mother living with two of her children (one has left)

Bilbao women at home: 4
Pepi, Laia, Monko, Marian
Age range: 23–29
Linked with parents: 4
Class background: 3 middle class, 1 working class

Bilbao men at home: 4
Vito, Bergante, Peru, José
Age range: 24–31
Linked with parents: 3
Class background: 3 middle class, 1 working class

Bilbao women away from home: 5
Julia, María, Oliva, Roja, Carlota
Age range: 22–28
Linked with parents: 4
Class background: 2 middle class, 3 working class

Bilbao men away from home: 5
Iñaki, Lapsus, Juan, Jon, Nacho
Age range: 26–32
Linked with parents: 4
Class background: 2 middle class, 3 working class

In the text we refer the respondents as follows:

Young people: name, location (B for Bilbao, L for Liverpool and T for Trondheim); age; gender; and living arrangements (LWP for living with parents and LH for left home). Parents: name, location as above, P to indicate parent, gender (of parent) and living arrangement of adult children (in some cases this may refer to more than one child).

The interviews were carried out by a local researcher in each city (two in Trondheim). Interviews with young people were divided into two parts. The first part centred on completing a life-history events matrix. Completion of the matrix enabled the interviewer to develop a brief biography of each respondent and helped frame the questions for the second part of the interview. This second part involved open-ended questions following an *aide mémoire* based around four themes: emotional issues related to leaving home/ living with parents; practical issues; implications for the young person; and, comparisons with others. Interviews with parents focused on in-depth questions only. Four *aide mémoires* were prepared for different types of respondents (young person living at home, young person left home, parent of young person living at home and parent of young person who has left home). We attempted to use the same *aide mémoires* in each country, although in practice we found that we had to adapt the themes and questions to reflect issues that were most pertinent to young people and parents in each country. For example, in Liverpool quite a few respondents talked at length about changes in funding for higher education. In Bilbao there was a lot of discussion about the inadequacy of state support but also of the importance of family solidarity.

During interviews respondents present a particular story or angle on their lives. They present themselves in a way that they feel appropriate for the purpose of the interview. Doing linked interviews (talking to young people, parents and other family members, for example, siblings and partners) gives a unique opportunity to explore this dimension of interviews but also raises important ethical issues about how to present the data. Parents and young people do not always give the same interpretation of recent events, aspirations and so forth. Examples of disparities between separate accounts include:

- General feelings about good or difficult relationships with parents. One respondent talked about a difficult time that she went through whilst living at home, following a break-up of a relationship; her parents did not mention this and thought that everything had been fine.
- Representations of 'responsibility'. In one instance, parents described their son as someone who 'lived for the moment', with no saving plans for the future, and expected him to remain living in the same area. The son talked about saving up for the future and wanting to leave the area where he grew up. He presented himself as more responsible than did his parents.
- Significance of relationships: One father said that his son had a girlfriend, the son made no mention of this.

In contrast, other linked interviews are mirror images of each other, with young person and parent singing from the same hymn sheet. While these different interpretations are intriguing, we need to be aware that we have to protect the confidentiality of each interview from other family members. For this reason we generally do not quote from two linked interviews, though we do summarize parents' and young people's responses.

Interviews were transcribed in the original language (all of the Basque interviews were carried out in Spanish). The Norwegian transcripts were then translated into English by one of the interviewers. The Spanish interviews were not translated and have been analysed in Spanish by one of the research team (Holdsworth) in collaboration with the interviewer. As a first stage in the analysis of the Spanish transcripts, a summary of each transcript was prepared in English; these summaries were cross-checked by the interviewer. During the course of the analysis important issues surrounding translation and the comparability of themes emerged. This is particularly relevant for analysis of respondents' discussions of *home, hjem* and *casa*. We have attempted to be sensitive to problems of direct translation, and have kept some of the flavour of the original interview in the translated quotations. We also gain a sense of the different ways in which language is used in the three counties: Spanish interviews are far longer than the British and Norwegian (shortest) ones, and this partly reflects different ways of expressing ideas and opinions. Rather than viewing these issues as obstacles to comparative research, we see that the advantage of this kind of approach is that it reveals not just how ideas are expressed differently in other contexts but also forces us as researchers to challenge some of our own preconceptions and assumptions about leaving home, independence and adulthood.

The analysis of qualitative interviews is a long, open-ended, business. We decided not to make use of any of the available computer packages, preferring to familiarize ourselves with the transcripts through repeated reading and discussion. We decided on seven broad headings (adulthood, ideas of home, economic independence, emotional independence, autonomy, family and generation, and state and policy) and analysed the transcripts around these themes. Repeated reading also helped us to identify particular narratives linking two or more of our chosen themes or potential case studies. Key quotations or illustrations of particular themes were extracted from the transcripts and placed together for easier access later on.

There are two further points that should be made about the process of analysis. The first is that it was very much a collaborative process. The three UK-based researchers (Holdsworth, Morgan and Patiniotis) had several shared discussions about the emerging themes. Holdsworth also had frequent discussions with our Spanish interviewer (Sara Barrón López) and both Holdsworth and Morgan had discussions with the two interviewers in Trondheim (Tor Erik Evjemo and Gjertrud Stordal). These discussions were not simply about technical problems of translation but also about different cultural meanings and understandings.

Second, there was a continuous dialogue between our developing theoretical and conceptual ideas and our readings of the transcripts. Thus, for example, our sense that the term 'generalized other' might be relevant emerged relatively late in the analysis process as a result of reading the transcripts. We then went back to Mead and his elaboration of the idea and then returned to think about our data with the aid of this idea. Other themes, of course, were present right at the beginning (ideas of independence, for example) but became refined and shaped through our various readings of the interviews. We have no illusions that we have obtained a complete picture. There are other themes to emerge or to be explored. In this way we find the interview transcripts 'good to think with'.

Our approach to the comparative is not to concentrate on the differences between the three locations but to work at different levels of abstraction. So, for example, we might compare within individual narratives and the contradictions that can be revealed within single accounts, or we might want to compare within families (although, as noted above, we have to be careful in doing so that we protect the anonymity of our respondents), as well as within locations and between locations. It is also useful to compare similar types of young people in different locations. For example we found very similar accounts from young women who lived with lone or solo-parenting mothers in each city. In the discussion of our analysis we follow the flow of this process of moving between different levels of comparison and, as appropriate, our discussions move between the differences between each location to more detailed analysis of individual case studies.

Concluding remarks

While we have been working on this project we have come to realize that 'leaving home' is a popular topic. Not only is it frequently the subject of discussion in the newspapers or radio and television but it is clearly something that is a matter of concern to many people and an important topic of discussion. Almost everyone, it seems, has a story to tell. There are stories of young people who are still living at home or who have returned home and there are anxieties expressed about young people who are abroad on a 'gap year'. There are frequent references to the cost of housing and comparisons made across generations. Some people refer to experiences in other countries, especially the widely reported phenomenon of the young men in Italy who seem more than content to remain at home.

The popularity of the topic should not come as a source of surprise because we are dealing with relationships between generations, specifically between parents and 'children'. A book, written by a leading family therapist, published in 1980 with the title *Leaving Home*, does not deal with the more material concerns that concern sociological researchers but uses the phrase as a kind of metaphor for or signifier of deeper psychological tensions across generations: 'When a young person succeeds outside the home, it is not merely a matter of individual success. He is simultaneously disengaging from a family, which can lead to consequences for the whole organization' (Haley, 1980: 30).

It is likely that much of the anxiety and interest that the topic of leaving home arouses reflects some of these deeper inter-generational dramas although for us, as social scientists, our focus of concern is elsewhere. Moreover, it would seem that the current concern does not simply reflect age-old tensions between parents and children but also wider anxieties about our own times and the abilities of young people in particular to handle the turbulences of modern life. Hence leaving the parental home can be seen as a point of convergence of a multiplicity of personal concerns and public issues.

We see here that the leaving-home process is not just a matter of concern for the individual making the transition but involves several other individuals and institutions as well. These include significant others such as parents, siblings, other kin and friends. At a more abstract level they also involve institutions (educational, the state, financial and so on) and markets. We have also found it useful to revive the concept of the 'generalized other' in order to indicate our young people's awareness that theirs is not simply an individual experience but something that is shared and shaped by the expectations of others, however shadowy these others may sometimes appear. Current notions of 'individualization' can be re-worked in order to take account of a recognition that these transitions are never just individual concerns. We would argue that it is essential that attempts are made to follow through this re-working.

The central significance of the leaving-home transition, therefore, lies in the fact that it has reverberations well beyond the individuals concerned. It is a social event that serves as a reminder of social connectedness, across generations, between individuals and between individuals and institutions. Also, as we hope to have shown in this theoretical review, it is a process that brings together some of the key concerns in sociological analysis: time, space, agency and structure, history and biography. In the following chapters we shall explore these theoretical and methodological inter-connections with reference to our specific themes.

3   Time and generation

Parents often talk about the younger generation as if they didn't have anything to do with it.

(Haim Ginott)

The process of leaving the parental home involves issues of both time and space. Issues of space will be the main focus of Chapter 4, but here the focus shifts to a consideration of more temporal themes. In this chapter we deal with these questions under the following three broad headings:

- notions of personal time, timetables and time-based practices;
- questions of the 'right' time to leave home;
- questions of historical time, the times in which the process of leaving home takes place.

It can be seen that these questions move outward from the day-to-day negotiations within the home, through broader cultural or normative questions, to wider themes of historical change.

These questions are linked to issues of space in a variety of ways. Notions of personal time may be linked to issues of personal space and the ability to do what one wishes to do in one's own time and one's own space. The question of the right time to leave home may be linked with subjective feelings of being overcrowded or under surveillance in the parental home or, in addition, the availability of alternative space. Questions of historical time are also linked, for example, to changing ideas of home, independence and household compositions. The focus in this chapter is on questions of time, but the themes discussed here are clearly linked to those discussed elsewhere in this book where we develop a more spatial orientation.

These discussions are clearly related to developing debates with sociology around the construction of time and time practices (Adam, 1990; Adam, 1995). Such debates consider, for example, different understandings of time (for example linear versus cyclical understandings) and different kinds of time (natural or bodily time, clock time, personal time, ritual time and so on). There are discussions of time as a resource and the negotiation of time within family (and other) practices. Other particular issues include the subjective experiences of time (time rushing by, time dragging) and the differences between households in terms of their 'time richness' or 'time poverty'. Differences in the experience or understandings of time may be mapped onto a variety of social divisions especially (in family contexts) gender and generation.

Within the domestic context there has been both policy-oriented and social scientific interest in the management of time. The increasing involvement of household and family members in institutions, organizations and practices outside the home has contributed to a greater focus on timetabling and the negotiation of time between partners and between parents and children. The fact that an increasing number of more-or-less individualized timetables require some measure of co-ordination gives the idea of negotiation particular salience as a metaphor and as a theoretical tool.

Personal time

As has been pointed out frequently, use of the term 'negotiation' does not rule out the possibility, indeed the likelihood, of inequalities in terms of power. Parties to the negotiation process have different resources and different negotiating skills derived from their positions within the family or from previous encounters. At the same time, negotiation within families is rarely, if ever, a zero-sum game and even the smallest infant has some measure of control over the activities of others. Indeed, modern family life is frequently characterized by an ideology of compromise and 'give and take' (Backett, 1982), which may begin at relatively early ages. This is often particularly marked in the case of time and its allocation between different family members where some degree of trading frequently takes place. What all this means is that within family practices individuals both possess personal timetables and, at the same time, are requested or required to take account of or be incorporated into the timetables of others.

We need to emphasize that, in the context of the present discussion, the negotiation of time is taking place between adults of different ages or, at the least, involving people who are on the verge of adulthood. In late modern societies, young adults are expected to, and wish to, move in and out of the parental home, exploring the worlds outside of education, work and, increasingly, leisure. Part of the process of becoming an adult involves the acquisition of new timetables that are not primarily determined or shaped by other family members within the parental home. However, the fact that many of them are continuing to live in the parental home means that an additional set of timetables needs to be taken into account and negotiated. The fact that the others within the household are also parents means that these negotiations take place in a context shaped by notions of parental obligations and responsibilities and emotional ties stretching back, in many cases, to infancy or earlier. It should be stressed that this negotiation of timetables takes place within a framework shaped by wider cultural and political ideas as to the nature and length of childhood, adult responsibilities and children's rights. In our Norwegian interviews, for example, there were several references to 'the little boy's room' and 'the little girl's room' and use of this phrase seemed to point to a notion of childhood time and space that both allowed children to be children while also developing a sense of independence.

Within the parental household there would seem to be two main points of conflict or negotiation. One is the question of mealtimes and the other is the more general one of time keeping, especially at night. Mealtimes, almost by definition, require some degree of temporal co-ordination; this is what distinguishes a meal from 'feeding'. They also continue to have some symbolic significance within family practices. Thus, from time to time, concerns are expressed about the decline of family eating in the context of increasing use of takeaways, fast food and microwaves (House of Commons Health Committee, 2004: 83), although it is likely that these concerns are exaggerated (McKendrick, 2004). The provision of food and the sharing of meals symbolizes, among other things, the provision of care and some sense of 'being a family'. Thus, when a young person has left home, he or she may continue to feel some obligation to attend a weekend or some ceremonial meal (for example, birthdays or Christmas) in the parental home. Conversely, one important sign of the changing status associated with leaving home is the ability to act as a host for one's own parents.

In our own data such issues were certainly mentioned but not with the frequency or the urgency that might be expected. Having to fit in with mealtimes was sometimes mentioned as a source of irritation, in all three contexts. This was one of the things that Bergante [B 31 M LWP] disliked about living at home. Adele [L 26 F LH] was expected to be home for her mother's cooked meals and Rachel [L 23 F LWP] felt that she was required to eat meals that were prepared while she was at home, even if she did not want them. However, some [for example Siv T 25 M LH] recalled having meals at home with some affection, although for others in all three countries the problem was removed through having separate cooking facilities. There are some brief accounts of returning to the parental home for meals after leaving home and, in Bilbao, there are descriptions of mothers continuing to prepare meals in Tupperware containers for their sons or daughters who have left home. Issues of food and mealtimes certainly crop up in the interviews but not as frequently as might have been supposed. These suppositions on the part of the researchers might, however, reflect generational or age-based differences as to the importance of meals and food.

The other area of time keeping, which was mentioned with much greater frequency, was to do with the time a young person was expected to return to the parental home after an evening or night out. This includes spending whole nights away from home. At a first glance, for most of the young people who we spoke to, this did not appear to be a major source of contention, certainly not in the period immediately prior to leaving the parental home. There seemed to be considerable evidence of negotiation around notions of 'reasonableness' and stress was often laid on the importance of keeping parents informed where there was some departure from an announced schedule. This was generally seen as reasonable on 'both sides'. Nevertheless, it is likely that the hours one observed or was required to observe constituted one sign of a more general sense of 'surveillance' that was seen as impinging upon a young person's sense of autonomy. For example, Anne Bente [T 25 F LH] said: 'they never did say during my teenager-years that I had to be at home, for example, ten o'clock.' Nevertheless she still felt that her behaviour was being monitored. A rather exotic example comes from Joar [T 28 M LH], who spent some of his teenage years on an island community and who recalls his parents listening for the sound of boats returning after a night's celebration.

It should be noted here that parental practices, and young people's responses to them, were not static. A common story was of the relaxation of parental controls as the young person approached maturity. Conflict, on the other hand, emerged where parents appeared to remain fixed at an earlier stage of childhood or where there was a conflict between different understandings of age and maturity.

There were, indeed, some young people who clearly resented control over their movements and in some cases this might have been a factor in the decision to leave home. Catherine [L 26 F LH] stated: 'You want to have freedom and you want to be able to come in at two o'clock in the morning, when you've gone out clubbing or whatever and, erm, you don't want your mother going "what time do you call this?" '

Kristin [T 21 F LH] recalls her parents asking her 'aren't you going to go to bed soon' and her parents expected her to call if she was going to be late, otherwise they would wait up for her. Laia [B 29 F LWP] felt that there was too much control in her parent's home, especially in relation to boyfriends and staying out all night. She admits to having lied to her parents about these questions on occasions.

It is interesting to note that three Norwegian accounts use a very similar phrase in talking about issues of time and time keeping in the parental home. Klara refers to 'different bio-rhythms' between herself and her daughter and the same phrase is used by Stian [T 26 M LWP], while Odd [T 26 M LH] refers to 'other time rhythms'. It is possible to argue that the use of a semi-scientific discourse here serves to remove an element of family conflict or power inequality so that it becomes a matter of mutual accommodation between equals rather than surveillance or the impositions of rules. This might be particularly important in a country with a strong egalitarian ethos (Gullestad, 1992).

Here, as elsewhere, it is difficult to isolate our discussion of time from questions of space (Wood and Beck, 1994: 3). It is not simply a question of the hours that a young person keeps; it is also one of where that young person is during those hours. This too enters into the negotiation process. Most respondents recognize that this is something that they are able to negotiate, but Bilbao respondents appear to have an easier time of this compared to their peers in Liverpool or Trondheim. This in part reflects climate differences (going out late is more feasible in Bilbao than in winter in Trondheim!) but more the traditions of Spanish life, which are ritualized through practices of 'la marcha' and 'fiesta'. However, young people in Trondheim celebrate 'russetid' (the last year at high school) by staying out all night whatever the weather and this ritual licence is accepted, perhaps reluctantly, by the parents.

The suggestion that issues of time keeping in particular and surveillance in general had more of a symbolic value (although one of considerable depth and complexity) is perhaps reflected in the interviews. There are few references to a sense of freedom once the individual has left the parental home, although it is likely that references to being able to do what one likes also means 'when one likes'. Lisa [L 25 F LWP] refers to 'staying up mega late' when she moved out as part of a list of newly enjoyed freedoms. But most seemed to find other constraints stemming from lack of resources and demands of work or others. Chris [L 29 M LH] notes, rather ruefully: 'it's just me on my own and there's just the telly for company . . . you don't know what to do with yourself sometimes.' Adele [L 26 F LH] sees her free evening being taken over by a 'stack of ironing' now that she has moved in with her partner and Ally [L 21 F LWP] felt regimented in her university hall of residence.

Linked to these discussions about the negotiation of time within the parental home are questions of domestic tasks and divisions of labour. This is to do with the allocation of time, although in complex ways. There is, by now, a large literature dealing with divisions of labour between adult partners (married couples, parents, cohabiting partners, gay and lesbian households: Dunne, 1998; Sullivan, 2000; Leonard, 2001) but relatively little dealing with divisions of labour between parents and children approaching adulthood (see, for example, Brannen et al., 2000 who discuss how household chores are viewed as a preparation for adult life). The data we have are impressionistic and often difficult to classify but the general picture to emerge from all three locations is one of relatively little input from the young adults whether we are considering those sections of the dwelling that are considered to belong to the young adult or other, more shared, areas. There would seem to be some gender differences, with girls being a little more willing to perform domestic tasks, although the differences are not all that striking. There is some indication of a greater degree of sharing of tasks in Norway and very little evidence of this in Spain. In the few examples where we have some information on the topic there is no evidence of this gendered division of labour changing much on leaving home.

Personal time can also be conceptualized as a resource and one that is often indirectly correlated to economic resources. Young people leaving home will impact on the dynamics of how this resource is distributed both for those who leave and those who are left behind. Parents, mainly mothers, might benefit from having less to do at home, with young people leaving experiencing the opposite. In fact some mothers did comment on the advantages of children leaving home in terms of the fact that they had less work to do after their children left. This was particularly so for non-working mothers, as working mothers were either more likely to employ domestic help (particularly in Bilbao) or were more successful in encouraging young people to help around the parental home.

To sum up, it can be said that questions to do with the use and control of time were, in the majority of cases, more-or-less resolved by the time young people left home. There were certainly some tensions and conflicts and in a few cases these may have contributed to the young person leaving home earlier than might have been expected. Constraints, or perceived constraints, over time were generally seen as part of a general sense of surveillance, perhaps to be expected as arising out of the tension between famialistic-based households and wider currents of individualization.

When to leave home: the 'right' time?

It is clear that now, as in the past, there are discernable patterns in the timing of leaving the parental home. Thus it is possible, within a given society, to say that, by a certain age, most people will have left the parental home and that before a certain age most young people will be within the parental home or its functional equivalent. Similarly, there are differences in terms of gender, social class and so forth, as outlined in Chapter 1. The question is whether such patterns can be associated with some normative notion of 'the right time' (Marini, 1984). It would seem to be the case, for example, that notions of the 'right' time to leave the parental home were more clearly defined for previous generations than they are for young people and their parents today. This was partly in terms of chronological age (and perhaps linked to clearer ideas of the 'age of majority') but more in terms of stage in the life-course. For women in particular, getting married was seen as being clearly the 'right' time to leave home. A young woman may 'live away' from home prior to this (Leonard, 1980) but with the clear expectation of a return to the parental home. For men, who tended to leave home at a later stage than women, marriage was also coupled with obtaining stable employment. These observations refer largely to Great Britain, especially between the middle of the nineteenth and twentieth centuries, although similar patterns might be found for other societies.

What is the right time now? Or, more pertinently, can we use the idea of the 'right' time with all its normative connotations in order to account for patterns within and differences between modern societies (Marini, 1984). The first point to note, as has already been shown, is that there is considerable variation between modern societies. Thus, in our comparative study, people left home at older ages in Bilbao (with women continuing to leave home in order to get married), at younger ages in Trondheim, with Liverpool somewhere in between. Liverpool has the widest range of variation among our respondents (though empirically countries such as Spain with older median ages at leaving tend to be more heterogeneous in terms of timing: Billari et al., 2001). The interesting theoretical question is the extent to which it is possible to read off norms as to the right time to leave home from these observed differences in practices. People may, in the course of an interview and in response to particular questions, refer to the idea of the 'right' time. This might be expressed in more general terms or, more likely, in relation to the particular immediate circumstances of a young adult at home or who has left the parental home, but it cannot be readily argued that the practices are based upon the norms; the reverse could easily be the case with the norms being deployed as a way of accounting for the practices. Leaving home, therefore, may be the occasion for the deployment of normative understandings and reflections and hence there may be affinities with other contexts and family practices where moral understandings are presented (Finch and Mason, 1993; Edwards and Gillies, 2003; Ribbens-McCarthy et al., 2003). Very often the most that one is able to say is in accordance with the statement of Lord Coleridge (quoted in Gluckman, 1964: 12):

> The Attorney-General has asked us where we are to draw the line. The answer is that it is not necessary to draw it at any precise point. It is enough for us to say that the present case is on the right side of any reasonable line that could be drawn.

In the course of our interviews various different ages were mentioned by both parents and young people. However, even while mentioning certain ages, the interviewees frequently also said that there was no clear norm and that it was either a question of circumstances or, more simply, 'up to the individual'. Rebecca [L 18 F LWP] provided a mixed response which is quite typical: 'There's not a right or a wrong time. There's a norm, like the average, what people do is leave to go to university . . . it depends on your personality . . .'

In some cases there might simply be a feeling that the young person is ready to leave or that it seemed to be 'the right time': 'I think you always know when it feels right' [Matthew L 24 M LH].

Kristin [T 21 F LH] referred to a 'sudden urge for freedom' and others refer to a time when it felt 'natural' to do so. Few of our respondents felt inclined to prescribe a 'right' age, but there was sometimes a sense of being 'too young' to leave or 'too old' to still be at home. A broad-brush picture would be that of 'individualization within limits' and although few seemed to be prepared to state these limits in terms of actual ages there was a sense of recognition when these limits had been breached. More generally, however, these quotations, with their references to 'freedom', 'your personality' or 'the individual', clearly draw upon a discourse of individualization.

Less obvious, perhaps, but also important is the way in which the quotations hint at different class locations. The complex relationships between social class, education and leaving home are discussed in Chapter 1. It is important, here, to remember that statements about generalities, what people normally tend to do, reflect different class locations. This can be seen, for example, when Rebecca in the quotation above refers to people leaving to go to university.

Reference to other life-course factors came up in all three locations. Adele [L 26 F LH] refers to moving on to 'the next stage in the relationship' and meeting a particular person also featured in some other accounts. References to marriage were, as might be expected, most common in Bilbao, whereas references to co-habitation were more frequent in the other two locations. Other aspects of a more expanded understanding of the life-course referred to completing full-time education, and there were several references to a material readiness. You ought to be in a position to buy a property in order to move and you should move if you are financially capable of moving. Robert [L 23 M LWP], for example, referred to 'getting proper money coming in'. Again we can see the class-based character of some of these observations.

The role of 'others' in the leaving home process is discussed in more detail in Chapter 7. However, it can be said that significant others (especially siblings or friends) occasionally provided role-models for some of our young people. These significant others sometimes merged into a kind of 'generalized other', a sense that everyone in a particular convoy or cohort was doing the same thing. Thus Hannah [L 29 F LH], who left home to get married, said 'so everybody was roughly doing the same type of thing' and Marc [L 21 M LWP] felt that 'we're at a weird age, when everyone's departing'. On the other hand, individuals might feel that they were behind or ahead of their particular set of friends or local cohort.

We found references to individualization, to the life-course and to the role of 'others' in all three locations. But what were the differences? Where ages were mentioned (although often with qualifications) the responses more-or-less paralleled the actual ages that applied in all three countries. In Liverpool the maximum age to be mentioned was 30 while others referred to 18, 18–22, 'at least 20' and 25. In Norway, one mother thought that 18 was a bit young and another felt that 27 was a little too old. Most suggestions clustered around the mid-20s. In Bilbao, 18 and 24 were 'too young' and the ages tended to be in the upper 20s with some mentions of 30.

In Norway (as we see in Chapter 5) there seemed to be a clearer tendency to link leaving home with attaining independence. This was clearly articulated by Marte [T 18 F LWP], who felt that you should not be dependent on your parents all the time otherwise 'you will face more trouble when you discover how the real world works'. Interestingly, there were several responses (more than occurred elsewhere) to the supposed or actual negative responses to those who were still at home past a 'normal' age. Friends might think it strange if you were still living at home. Andrea [T 27 F LH] referred to a young man she had met in Oslo who was still living in the parental home and wondered whether 'he might be one of those mummy's boys'. This was one of the strongest expressions of disapproval, although a diffuse sense of anxiety about remaining home was to be found in some other accounts.

Bilbao respondents produced some of the most distinctive responses. As has already been mentioned, there was a recognition, here as elsewhere, that age was not the issue so much as 'occasion' or 'circumstances'. And while 'circumstances' in the other two locations might be interpreted in more individualistic terms, here the references were more structured. In fact, the key reference was to marriage. This, according to Julia [B 29 F LH] was the 'Spanish system'. Pepi [B 28 F LWP] also mentioned marriage while stating to the interviewer that she might be seen as a little 'old-fashioned' in her views. One interesting argument put forward by one set of parents was that it was no longer necessary to leave home in order to have sex. Such a straightforward recognition of sex before marriage, perhaps even within the parental home, was rare however. What was clear across most of the accounts was that leaving home in order to live with friends was not conforming to what was expected and this was even more the case when it came to leaving home in order to live alone.

The ideal seemed to be to leave home without conflict or without causing distress to parents. Where the leaving-home process did 'go wrong' there was a source of considerable unhappiness in some cases (see also Jones, 1995). Yet it would be wrong to account for this simply in terms of Spanish 'familialism' and it leave it at that. Parental accounts betrayed some contradictory emotions to the extent that it was possible to talk of the 'parental paradox' in Spain. On the one hand there was a desire for young people to stay at home until they were ready to leave, ideally in order to get married. Nevertheless, there were also some references to young people treating the parental home as an 'hotel' (more so than in the two other locations) and a certain amount of teasing or joking about the 30-year-olds who were still at home. Some suggested that young people were scared, lazy or just too comfortable to move. In some cases, parents felt that young people might be using the cost of housing or the state of the labour market as an excuse for staying at home. Yet, at the same time, these accounts remained at a joking level. Overall, parents' attitudes and actions indicated that they were always willing to provide food, accommodation and support for their offspring of whatever age.

We have suggested, following Lord Coleridge, that while there were few clear statements of the 'right' age to leave home, there was some awareness as to when the flexible boundaries had been breached. Hence it is illuminating to consider some 'deviant' cases. Outside of the parental jokes about hotels we did not find anyone in Bilbao who felt that they had left it too late to leave home. In Trondheim we have already noted how young people over the age of, roughly, 25 felt that they might be the object of adverse comments on the part of others. Particular circumstances might explain a 'late' departure. Hilde [T 27 F LWP] had already left home but returned home to be with her parents after the tragic death of her sister. But it was clear that she saw this as a temporary arrangement. Yvonne [T 26 F LWP] similarly had left home to live with a boyfriend but returned after this relationship ended. Further, she was living with her widowed father and it is possible that her sense of obligation delayed her further departure from the parental home.

Perhaps the most striking example of someone living in the parental home was Lynn [L 35 F LWP]. She recognizes that this might be seen as abnormal: 'I know there's a stigma about people living at home, you know, at my age.' She compares her situation with her married friends who have children but states that they are more jealous of her than she is of them. Nevertheless, she regrets not having children. Another reference group here are the people in the office where she works. Here she is the youngest person in the office and this plus the fact that she has remained single made her feel that the others 'talk down' to her. She lives with her mother, reasonably amicably it would seem, and the main rule Lynn is expected to adhere to is to go outside for a cigarette. Lynn's account is a good example of the way in which actual others and generalized others might be co-opted in order to provide an understanding of her particular status.

The clearest case of early leaving in Trondheim was Joar [T 28 M LH] who left home at the age of 16. However, he was living on a small island at the time and moved in order to go to high school. Then he stayed with his uncle, leaving into his own apartment at around the age of 18. Although he recognizes that his experience was probably rather unusual, he does not feel that he has lost anything and talks of a continuing good relationship with his parents (see Chapter 7 where Joar's experiences are discussed in more detail). The mother of Kristin [T 21 F LH] expressed some reservations about her daughter's departure, although this was more a reflection of her concerns about her daughter's pregnancy than her actually leaving home. Generally, parents were more likely to express doubts about 'early' leaving than the young people themselves.

In Liverpool the youngest cases were problematic in a variety of ways. Helen was in a foster home when she was interviewed at the age of 17. She 'never' got on with her stepfather and did not see her biological father. She had also experienced an attempted rape by her sister's boyfriend. She experienced a variety of temporary addresses before her present foster home. Sharon was 21 at the time of the interview and had left her foster home at 17. She wanted to be independent and had argued with her foster parents about time keeping. She now lives in a local authority flat.

From a British perspective, the Spanish 'early leavers' did not seem to be so problematic. However, they were clearly seen this way in their particular contexts. Roja [B 23 F LH] was living with friends in rented accommodation. She was employed as a draftsperson. Her mother clearly thought that she left too soon and in the 'wrong' way and Roja also recognizes her situation as unusual. She states that she misses her parents and goes home to them every weekend. (Her parents claim that she left because she didn't want to contribute to the household budget.) Olivia was 22 and a student, also working part-time and living with friends. She had some serious arguments with her father (still painful to recall), which seemed to be about behaviour at home in relation to time keeping and other matters. Her mother calls her every day. Lapsus [B 27 M LH], while not an early leaver, left home to live with friends against his parents', and especially his mother's, wishes, and recounts how difficult this was for his mother and that she had cried and had become depressed. This did not prevent him from leaving, but it was something that he had to negotiate during the process of leaving. In all these cases (and in one or two other earlier leavers) there was a sense of some kind of family breach, sometimes combined with a desire to repair the damage and to maintain contact.

To conclude this section it could be said that a broadly individualistic discourse dominates discussions of the 'right time', especially when it comes to specifying a particular age. However, variations occur when we look at circumstances, more structured and related to the life-course in the Spanish context, and more individualistic in the other two locations. Yet while it was 'up to the individual', individuals rarely made their move without reference to significant others (family and friends) or to more diffuse constructions of the generalized other. Norms may be seen more in terms of ways of accounting for actions already taken but the norms themselves are not necessarily random. Some accounts may be more legitimate than others.

Historical time and generations

Much of the argument in this book is devoted to showing that leaving the parental home is not a natural (or even inevitable) process and that the decision to leave home (or not to leave home) is influenced by all kinds of factors in addition to the particular personalities or domestic situations of the individuals most immediately involved. These factors may be quite specific (such as those to do with particular changes in welfare policies or the state of the housing market) or much more general (such as long-term restructuring of the labour market or 'individualization'). Such historical factors rarely, if ever, bear down in some deterministic fashion on the individuals involved but they are an important part of the framework of understanding. Further, such understandings enter into the accounts of our respondents who frequently refer to issues to do with housing and the labour market and, occasionally, to themes such as individualization.

The ways in which young people and their parents develop some understanding of historical change and their position in it are of particular interest to us. One idea that may be especially helpful here is that of 'generation'. Here we are primarily concerned with understandings of generation from the perspectives of the young people and their parents – that is with references to 'my generation', 'my parents' generation' and so on. Given the family context that is the focus of interest here (and in several other studies) this use of generation is hardly surprising because part of an understanding of family practices is that it involves people of different generations not necessarily located within the same household (Scott, 2000).

However, it is important to note the ways in which these generations are actively constructed rather than simply existing as some determining force. In the first place, our interview samples include people within a relatively wide age range (wider than in some similar studies) so that the historical circumstances to which different generations refer will themselves be quite different. Second, there is always some element of generalization and elaboration involved whenever individuals talk about, say, my generation or my parents' generation. Put simply, it is relatively rare for parents to tell their children 'how it was' in their generation as some simple straightforward narrative. Most likely, we are referring to odd remarks, family stories and responses to direct questions that may be blended with newspaper or television accounts or, indeed, with what is learned at school or college. 'My parents' generation' may have some features in common with the 'generalized other' discussed earlier.

One theme that emerged from the interviews, prompted through questioning, was the difference between the experiences of the present generation and those of the parents, or sometimes earlier, generations. Points of comparison were made with reference to a number of different dimensions, such as economic factors, educational opportunities as well as changing attitudes to marriage, cohabitation and sex. Few, if any, thought that there was any clear continuity in respect to these issues. However these constructions of generational difference could not be readily classified into 'better' or 'worse'. In other words, if we take an overview of the totality of young people's experiences (rather than just focusing on the economic, for example) there was no clear-cut agreement as to whether young people had an easier or more difficult time today as compared to when their parents were of a similar age. The young people in Liverpool seemed to be fairly evenly divided on this issue and it did not seem to make much of a difference whether they had left or were still living at home. However, there was some tendency for parents to think that times were easier in their generation. (This is perhaps contrary to popular stereotypes of parents claiming that young people have it too easy today.) Norwegian young people were more inclined to see things as better now with parents having a more complex or mixed view.

Views seemed to be most complex in Bilbao where there were clear understandings that things were different between the generations although there was considerable uncertainty as to whether things were better now or then. There was some tendency, perhaps more so among the parents, to argue that young people had an easier time now although the differences were not striking. Monko [B 23 F LWP] gave an account that pointed to some of the cross currents when it came to evaluating the present against the past. Her mother married when she was 21 or 22. She recognizes that things have changed and wonders whether this has been for the better or for the worse. It was not, she argued, that young people today did not have a sense of urgency but they had become accustomed to, and happy with, living in the parental home. At the same time she recognizes that there is another group of young people who stay at home for economic reasons.

In Spain the fact of regime change (Franco died in 1975) helped to shape a clearer sense of 'then' and 'now'. When the parents talk about change they are not simply talking about changes in personal circumstances but also a wider sense of social change. There are closer linkages between the political and the personal in these Spanish accounts. There is some recognition of political and economic change in the other interviews (especially Liverpool) but the sense of the past as another country was stronger in the Spanish responses.

In all three locations a sense of change was seen firstly in terms of family. Again, this was clearest in Bilbao, where nearly all the respondents reported parents leaving home to get married at a significantly earlier age than at present. In those cases where this did not take place, there was a recognition that the circumstances were unusual. In Liverpool, and to a lesser extent in Trondheim, there were frequent references to the 'normal', usually early, life-cycle transitions:

Get married, and have children and be a housewife. [Adele L 26 F LH]

When they were my age, they were married, and that made their situation quite different from mine . . . [Odd T 26 M LH]

My mother was 19 years old I think, and my father was 21 years old I think . . . married and expecting children, and you might say the entire package at that young age . . . [Ben T 26 M LWP]

like my mum and dad were like nineteen and seventeen, I think, when they got married, like and they had my sister straight away and that. [Robert L 23 M LWP]

Some linked this with getting a new house:

They erm, I think what it was, I mean they both, they met when they were young, I think they were about 18 . . . And they erm . . . I suppose started a relationship then. They got married when they were twenty-one, and I think up until then they both lived with their parents. And then erm, yeah, it was really kind of neat, you know. And then they got this place, you know. [Matthew L 24 M LH]

One set of parents present a similar picture:

We were married at twenty-one and living here with a mortgage. By the time we were [our son's] age, you know, I was not pregnant, but we were thinking of starting a family. And you know, we'd moved away, and so, yeah, you've got to be aware of that really. [Andrea, married to Paul, L P]

Rita and Tom [L P LWP], another set of parents, saw it as 'just part of life' and that 'You just sort of get a job and you get married.' They, in common with some other parents and young people, noted that there was no cohabitation in 'those days'.

There were, of course, some deviations from the standard model. Neil's [L 21 M LWP] parents had been together since they were 15 but in the intervening period they got divorced and re-married each other. Nina's [L 24 F LWP] mother left home because 'she fell pregnant':

She was working sort of in an office at the time, and she was eighteen, fell pregnant, left home to live with my biological father, who is now sort of no longer with us . . . yes, they got a mortgage together . . . when she was pregnant with my older brother, and then fell pregnant with me when she was twenty-one.

There were references to co-habitation in the parents' generation in Trondheim and to some, by British standards, non-standard transitions:

> Well, you know, I did marry when I was [27] . . . after quite a strong pressure actually [laughter] . . . you must get married because number two is on the way . . . [Oddvar, T P]

Generally there seemed to be a shared understanding between parents and young people that things were different then and that there was more-or-less a standard model that was followed, with some variations, by most of the parents. We can also see, in some of these accounts, attempts to link the parents' experiences with a more general understanding of family change over one generation.

Evaluations of whether things were better then or now can be expressed, largely, in terms of employment and housing. Some of the Liverpool respondents were quite clear that the labour market was much easier when they were younger. As one father remarks, 'we were the last generation to leave school and be guaranteed a job' [Peter, L P LWP]. And such transitions from school to employment were more straightforward. As Kate, Peter's partner, remarks:

> I mean because all the people I went to school with you could just get any job you wanted really. You know if you decided you wanted to work in a bank, you just wrote to them, and chose which one was the best place, the best job . . . [Kate L P LWP]

To another father it was hard work (begun at the age of 15) but the particular job had been determined by his father, having had the job recommended by a friend. Simon [L 21 M LWP] also referred to the apparent ease of getting a job in 'those days': 'And they said back then it was a lot easier to walk out of a job in the morning and go into another one in the afternoon.'

It has to be remembered that these are constructions, based on personal experiences or reported experiences, and that undoubtedly a lot of smoothing over of reality is taking place. Moreover, this sense of simplicity in terms of economic factors is not just restricted to the apparent ease of getting a job but includes young people's own expectations and consumption patterns. This comparison of consumption patterns is commented on by quite a few parents, as Quijote from Bilbao and Mary from Liverpool describe:

> In our case we had it easier because in my time households were simple households, not great houses . . . I think that they [young people] ask for a little more. They ask for a little more, and they have the right [to do so] . . . It is difficult for everybody to leave for worse, as

it was difficult for us. We used to leave home because we used to think, rightly or wrongly, we left for the better. [Quijote, B P LWP]

When I got married I can honestly say, I've never borrowed anything from my parents, never. They didn't have it to lend, anyway. Erm, and we bought, when we first got married, we had a flat. And we were married three years before we moved into here. Into this house; we saved up. And we started to buy this place, and erm, at [daughter]'s age, I had a house, and the house was all furnished. [Mary L P LWP]

Again the pattern is broadly similar in Trondheim: Sissel [T P F LH] noted that 'overall it was much cheaper to leave and to get a place for yourself then', although there were some suggestions that expectations were lower in the past. Marianne, a mother, recalls living in a small apartment with two small children and a toilet in the basement. They showered at their parents-in-law's place.

There were, therefore, references to employment and housing and the general impression conveyed is that matters were easier in the past. However, that is not the whole story and inter-generational comparisons wrestled with more complex and ambiguous moral evaluations. In part this was, as might be expected, a comparison between the more restricted earlier times and the freer present. Liverpool respondents made several references to 'strictness' and 'old-fashioned' attitudes in the past which bore particularly on young women. Sarah [L 21 F LH], speaking of her mother, said: 'But there was no idea of going off and doing this, that and the other at all. My Mum especially had a very strict convent upbringing.'

In Norway these references tended to revolve around cohabitation and expectations to get married and similarly sexual freedom was sometimes referred to in Bilbao. Moreover, in Bilbao many parents emphasized how their relationships with their own children were very different from the way in which their parents had treated them, and that parent-adult child relations were based on friendship rather than discipline and control. However there was some questioning, chiefly or perhaps exclusively by the parents, as to whether matters had gone 'too far' in terms of the freedom of the young.

A fairly common construction, across all three locations, was in terms of a contrast between the relatively simpler earlier times and the complexities facing present generations. This could be seen as the familiar argument that relative lack of choice made for an easier life while the openness of modern life (partly brought about through the expansion of higher education) produces a state somewhat akin to anomie. Marc [L 22 M LWP] recognizes some of these complexities:

You'd like to say, oh, it was much easier for them then, and that sort of thing. I think we get more opportunities. We just don't take them.

There was probably less opportunities to do all thousands of different – because new industries are popping up every one to five years, aren't they? . . . So we – we do have, we've got a lot more choice. But we don't take them, take the opportunities, as well as they do.

Others, in all three locations, referred to the growing experience of (and acceptance of) debt in the early stages of life and the higher expectations, again partially brought about through higher education.

It has to be recognized that we are dealing (in the case of the young people's accounts) with second-order constructions of the past, and their parents' pasts in particular. Young people often profess ignorance as to the timing and circumstances of their parents' leaving home. Some qualified their remarks with words like 'I think', while others confessed more-or-less complete ignorance:

> Well . . . I do sort of know, but its not crystal clear. I mean, I think she lived with a few different people, had a few flats, and then she went back home as well. I'm not really sure. [Rachel L 23 F LWP]

> Dad, no. I don't have a clue about how he left home . . . I think, it might have been marriage. But I don't, oh, I think it was possibly marriage, like when she married dad . . . So I don't know, I don't know. But my gut instinct was they used to say that she left home when she got married(laughs). [Rebecca L 18 F LWP]

These professions of ignorance were rarer among Spanish respondents. This may be explained in part because there is less doubt about leaving home to get married, as this is what most young people expect to do today, as they did in the past.

As an illustration of the complexity of inter-generational understanding let us, first, consider Paula, a single parent from Liverpool with four children. Aged between 13 and 28, two of her children have left home, but the youngest and oldest have not. This longish extract from the transcript gives a flavour not only of her particular situation but of her construction of generations:

> I gave them their freedom because I was brought up different – my father was very strict. And I didn't want to be like that with mine. And the one thing I did notice was I spoilt them in certain ways, I suppose I was trying to make up for giving them a rubbish father.
>
> I didn't want my kids to be brought up like me, my father was really strict. And you rebel. And that's what I did when I left home at 14, and I never went back home from that day, because the restrictions pushed me away.

And that now comes into the next generation, doesn't it, now my kids think 'well, me mother had us young, look how we've struggled. I don't want that for my child.' And that's what stops them from having kids.

This is interesting in that it is a three-generation story, told by the woman in the middle. In a kind of popular Freudian (or Philip Larkinesque) account there is a chain of causality running across the generations here. A strict father leads to teenage rebellion, pregnancy and a 'rubbish' partner. This leads to some amount of 'spoiling' of the present generation within the context of some perceived struggle which 'causes' the children to be turned off parenthood altogether. This is not, however, a complete denial of agency. Paula works hard to try to make up for what she sees as her children's unfortunate start in life. This is an individual account but it is likely that it draws upon some more public discourses such as the idea of a move from strict controls to permissiveness.

In Bilbao, Bergante is 31 and living at home. His parents speculate on the differences between their generation and Bergante's experiences. They point to the familiar demographic facts that young people today are marrying later, having children later and having fewer children. When they were Bergante's age they had left home, married and had three children. When they left home, they had fewer expectations and saw the parents of their own parents' generation as being inflexible and traditional. However, this is not necessarily progress. There is the potential that today the parental home may be treated like a hotel without charge for young people. They are comfortable there and do not do much to contribute to the running of the house. Young people today do not have a timetable and come and go as they please. Bergante's parents provide a clear expression of the ambivalence experienced by many Spanish parents, expressing this partially in generational terms.

Finally, these extracts from the interview with Klara (a mother in Trondheim) show a different kind of ambivalence. Her daughter has just left home and is expecting a baby with her cohabiting boyfriend. She states that she was 'quite mature' (40) when her daughter was born. She draws upon her own past to understand her daughter, who has just left home: 'but I also know now that she is enjoying have a place of her own, and that is something that you remember from your own youth . . . the stimulus you get when you have left your parents' home, you know . . .'

She had been a student herself and left home at the age of 20. Her partner and her went to Oslo to live in a small flat, later marrying: '. . . so after all, I do think that it is healthy that they leave in a way and get to feel what life is all about so to speak . . .' Accommodation then was limited and expensive and co-habitation was rare.

On the whole her approach is in favour of the changes that have taken place. She feels that today's society is more honest in a way and that people do things because they want to rather than because of tradition. But the pressures were probably easier for her and her husband to bear: 'things were more conservative in a way . . . having all sorts of rules and us young people more inclined to obey rules . . . we didn't have the guts to question what our parents told us . . .'

Subtly, this evaluation moves into a more questioning attitude to the modern generation:

> Nowadays, I get the impression that many youngsters have their own agenda, not caring so much on what their parents or the society says or experts so to speak . . . This is something that certainly was not the case when I was young.

> . . . there are times when I feel that today's youngsters don't want us parents to ask so many questions and in a way, being controlling so to speak . . .

> . . . yes, I do have the feeling that some people today too easily get themselves involved in cohabitation, so to say . . . and ending it being no big matter, either, you know . . . I have problems with understanding the easiness with which this is often being done in today's society so to speak, from an emotional point of view, you know . . . Many more people nowadays are breaking up than it used to be during my youth so to speak . . .

As in some of the other interviews with parents, this ambivalence, expressed in generational terms, is conducted as a kind of moral debate within herself in response to the interviewer. It is also worth stressing that these accounts are also filtered through social class as well as national differences. Paula is more clearly working class and her sense of unease about her children's experiences reflects wider discourses about the impact of poverty and lone parenthood on children (Duncan and Edwards, 1999), whereas the other two accounts are middle class.

Concluding remarks

We can see the importance of 'personal' time as a theme underlying the transition out of the parental home. Personal time could become an issue in the parental home and was the subject of some negotiation. Part of the attraction of leaving home was the possibility of having relative freedom to come and go as one pleased, part of the more negative understanding of 'independence'.

To some extent this expectation was illusory, however, especially where the move was into some form of shared accommodation, either with a partner or a set of friends or students. Time is always a matter for negotiation when there is more than one person in a household. It is at these points that we see the close inter-dependence of time and space.

Notions of the 'right time' to move also seem to be more matters of negotiation rather than normative prescription. In Trondheim and Liverpool there were not any clear ideas that women (in particular) should leave home to get married or that either men or women should leave home for employment. However, it should not be thought that there was complete freedom in this matter. There were some notions (especially among parents) about individuals being too young or not ready to leave home just as there were generalized notions about the inappropriateness of remaining home when many of ones peers had already left. In Bilbao, as we have seen, the idea that both women and men should leave home to get married remained strong.

Individuals, both parents and young people, had a broad generational understanding of how things had changed. The picture of the parental generation was one where people left home in order to get married and where transitions out of the parental home were linked, not only to marriage, but also to full-time employment and affordable housing. Some young people had a relatively hazy understanding of the circumstances surrounding their parents' moves out of the parental home, but most were able to combine their own family understandings with wider notions of historical change. This possibly reflects the fact that these issues and their own experiences are now more likely to be matters of public debate in the media. Leaving home, in common with other transitions, provides an occasion for these inter-generational comparisons. These comparisons are not simply to do with individuals or individual families but also the understandings and experience of historical change mediated through generational relationships.

The socially constructed nature of 'generations' comes clearly through these accounts. Although we, as researchers, invited the respondents to speculate about generational differences it is likely that people do routinely seek to make sense of where they are now in terms of comparisons of this kind. In the process of doing this 'generational work' they are also constructing the very generations to which they are referring. Further, such generational material is also shaped by class differences (as we see in the cases cited above) and gender. Thus, for example, there seems to be a general agreement that things have improved for women despite some possible doubts about individualization. Nevertheless, generation should be seen as one of the major ways in which individuals make meaningful connections between their own lives and historical change and the time of leaving home provides one appropriate opportunity for speculation about these changes.

4 Home

When I speak of home, I speak of the place where, in default of a better, those I love are gathered together; and if that place were a gypsy's tent, or a barn, I should call it by the same good name notwithstanding.

(Charles Dickens, *Nicholas Nickleby*)

In order to contextualize experiences of leaving home, it is appropriate to consider the places young people are leaving and moving to. In this chapter we turn our attention more directly to the spatial aspects of leaving home transitions. The chapter is divided into three sections, which address the following themes and questions:

- Where is home? How do young people and parents make sense of the varied ways in which we might define where home is?
- Meanings of home and how these map onto a theoretical understanding of the production of space.
- How young people go about creating homes through the processes of leaving home.

Having a home, or a place of shelter, is a fundamental human right and an essential element of human existence: 'For Heidegger, dwelling . . . means to reside or to stay, to dwell at peace, to be content or at home in a place. It is the manner in which humans inhabit the earth' (Urry, 2000: 131). The centrality of home is such that, for most people, it is something that we take for granted. Yet, in practice, human existence is usually characterized by multiple 'homes' that may either reflect different scales (a house, a neighbourhood, a city, a region, a country) or different locations as people move to new homes, in the same or different neighbourhood, city, region or country. Individuals' experiences and understandings of home life may be held up to greater assessment or reconsideration at points of crisis or transition where the everyday flow of domestic life is disrupted. Unpacking meanings of home around a point of transition therefore allows us to explore how breaks in continuity are key to unravelling experiences of a place (Milligan, 1998: 9).

The process of leaving home is one such uprooting that potentially raises intriguing questions surrounding young people's experience of home, about its location and well as its significance for their sense of belonging and identity. Similar studies of meanings and attachment to home have used other discontinuities such as the invasion of domestic space as in the case of burglary (Korosec-Serfaty, 1985; Chapman, 1999) and the experiences of transnational migrants (Levitt and Waters, 2002; Ahmed et al., 2003). For the latter the tensions of attachment to conflicting home spaces and the multi-layered scaling of home – where home can be a house, village, community or country – raise important questions about the relationship between lived and imagined homes in places of arrival and origin. Questions about how trans-national migrants experience belonging to two (or more) home places simultaneously and the implications for the supposed universality of home spaces are analogous to the themes explored in our study of leaving home.

Where/what is home?

As home is the most obviously spatial of our key themes, it is appropriate to begin with considering more overtly geographical questions about the identification (what) and location (where) of home. For the overwhelming majority of our subjects in Liverpool and Trondheim, home and *hjem*[1] (Norwegian) were not difficult topics. In contrast to other issues raised in the interviews (such as adulthood) young people and parents alike often spoke at length about home with little hesitation and considerable thoughtfulness and elaboration. For some of our Liverpool subjects, home appeared to be part of an on-going discussion, for example Marc describes conversations with his father about the location of home:

> I did actually ask my dad this the other day; well, not the other day, it was a few months ago, back now. This has been my home for basically as long as I can remember, it's been my home. But I said to; I said to him, what do you class as home? It was actually that question, I said where is home? [Marc L 22 M LWP]

Marc's reflections on where home is are also about identity and the importance of home and belonging. Yet the ease and familiarity that Marc

---

[1] Because of the difficulties in translating the various words used to refer to home in the interviews, particularly in Spanish, we do not translate *hjem* (home), *casa* (house/home), *hogar* (hearth/home) or *pueblo* (village/neighbourhood).

shows when talking about home provide a striking contrast to respondents' initial reaction in Bilbao. This reflects, at least initially, Sopher's argument of the peculiarity of the English home. The English word home has few equivalents in other languages, particularly Romance languages. According to Sopher (1978: 262):

'Home' is a peculiarly English concept, although some of its properties appear in the other Germanic languages . . . English 'home' is elastic in scale and implies some social permeability; the Romance terms that stand for different scale connotations of home are closed spaces, each located at a fairly well-defined scale.

The essence of the idea of the English home is its multiplicity of meaning and the sense of 'warmth, security, and intimacy of relationships' that are attached to both home as family dwelling and home places. Sopher suggests that this linguistic segregation is related to different conceptualizations of space, with a more open and fluid conceptualization in English speaking countries, compared to more bounded conceptions of space in Mediterranean countries.

Discussions about *casa* (Spanish) often began hesitantly and many respondents found the question 'what does *casa* mean for you?' problematic in that, when expressed in Spanish, the question sounded unusual and rather strange. In the interviews there is much discussion about the appropriate word for home, either *casa* (home/house) or *hogar* (home/hearth) and that, rather than responding positively, many respondents repeated the question, as if trying to work out what it actually meant, as Marian's response illustrates:

Interviewer: What does the idea of *casa* mean for you?
Marian: The idea of *casa*? A *casa*?
Interviewer: A *casa* or *casa* . . . *hogar* or everything that you associate . . .
Marian: Well! The idea of *casa* is *hogar* for me. Well the place that is yours, your enclosed place, your . . . I don't know . . . your . . . *casa*, I don't know, I don't know; or it could be . . . [Marian B 28 F LWP]

As this example illustrates, the distinction between *casa* and *hogar* is blurred. *Hogar* may be used to express emotional and relational qualities of home, but it does not have the physical embodiment that *casa* implies. *Casa* can imply family, however, in the sense of belonging to a *casa* (analogous to the use of 'house' by English aristocratic families), though this is not necessarily dependent on co-residence (Bestard Camps and Contreras Hernández, 1997: 72). These distinctions between the physical *casa* and the emotional *hogar* are made by a number of respondents, both parents and young people:

Casa is where I live and *hogar* I see as more like, more with family, with family and the children. [Rosa B P LH]

Hogar for me is more about family, parents, children . . . But my *casa* is *casa*. Where I'm living . . . [Lapsus B 26 M LH]

You buy a *casa* and then soon . . . in this *casa* your create your *hogar* and you create your life . . . *hogar* is the place where . . . you live. [Vito B 28 M LWP]

Hence, rather than endorsing Sopher's distinctness of the English home we argue that in Spanish the lexical distinction between *casa* and *hogar* incorporates different meanings and ways of conceptualizing 'home'. Once our respondents realized that by 'home' we were referring to both *casa* and *hogar* they warmed to the subject.

Returning to Marc's discussion about talking to his father about where home is, we need to recognize that home rarely is a unique place, nor is it necessarily where we usually reside. Phenomenological writings on the landscapes of home take the dialectics of home/journey (Tuan, 1974), home/anti-home (Sopher, 1979), home/non-home (Porteous, 1976), as the fundamental experience of space. This dialectic does emerge is some accounts when young people talk about their experiences of leaving home but also staying at home. It is, as Dorothy experienced in *The Wizard of Oz*, that one has to leave home to get a sense of what home means. For example, Martin is a student at Liverpool who lives with his parent. He is a first-generation student with no family experience of leaving home to go to university and it never really occurred to him to leave. The choice to stay at home is more common among students from Martin's background (Patiniotis and Holdsworth, 2005), yet also reflects a localized working-class perspective, which impacts on his sense of home: 'It's . . . as being, as like there's never been nowhere else where I've lived. So I've no other ideas in my head about what home would be' [Martin L 21 M LWP].

Martin's account would appear to endorse a dialectical approach, although in a negative sense as his absence of home is because he has never experienced anywhere else. Other respondents who talked about the contrast between journeying away from home and being at home did so in the sense that the journey was through a series of homes or home-like situations rather than a stable base against which the movement was measured. It is more appropriate to understand the dialectic of home in terms of many journeys between different manifestations and meanings of homes, rather than a more fixed movement between home and anti-home. In other words the sense of home can be ascribed to many different places. We might talk about a place 'feeling like home' or talk about a 'home from home'. Sometimes these feeling are only partial, but these shades of grey are more common than a fixed idea of what is and what is not a home.

Rather than oppositions to home, the concept of competing homes was referred to by a number of young people, particularly among those who had temporarily left home, such as students. For example, in all three countries young people distinguished between 'home' and 'home home' with the latter referring to the parental home (Heath and Cleaver, 2003). This sense of alternative home spaces was not thought particularly problematic or destabilizing. As Gareth, a middle-class second-generation Liverpool student who has 'left home' describes, there is rarely any confusion as to which 'home' young people are referring to:

> Well, there's kind of a thing amongst students that we had kind of made up our own words. So 'home home' is where you're from, like Essex, and 'home' is Liverpool. It's like when you see someone at the bus stop saying, I'm going home, every time – well, what do you mean? 'Home', or 'home home'? And it's kind of a weird thing amongst students that nobody realizes they're saying it, but everybody knows immediately what – what you mean. [Gareth L 22 M LH].

Returning to Sopher's claim that essentially the English home incorporates a far more fluid spatiality than Romance terms, we found that this sense of different spatial boundaries was not unique among British, or even Norwegian, respondents. Juan, for example, reflects on a wider understanding of where home is than the dwelling where he actually lives:

> *Casa* ... it is what you see here now ... no it is more ... much more than four walls. My *pueblo* is my *casa*! It could be, the *pueblo* where I live. And I feel that it is my *casa* and for that reason, yes, I am determined not to leave ... that is where I live. It is my *pueblo* ... It very much suits me here ... perhaps I can live anywhere! [Juan B 30 M LH]

Juan's debate or indecision may also be seen as representing the ambiguity around the idea of home, between a particular residence or household and a locality or region, which can itself be defined in broad or narrow terms. These two meanings have, some might argue, diverged in modern times (Gullestad, 1992: 51) and generally we find the more narrow spatial reference prevailing in our accounts. If there has been a divergence (although not a complete one) between the wider and the narrower understandings of home, the opposite may have been true in relation to the home/family distinction where there appears to be a growing convergence (Hareven, 1991: 254). Certainly, the overlap between family and home is considerable in many of our accounts. As discussed above, many respondents in Bilbao deployed the *hogar* for family/ *casa* for house distinction.

Concepts of 'home' are also situational, as another Spanish young person, Nacho [B 28 M LH] describes. Where home is very much depends on where he is and he recognizes a hierarchy of homes: 'it depends where I am! If I am in Andalucía my *casa* is in Algorta, Bilbao, Bizkaia, but if I am in England, my *casa* is in Spain . . . and I am not particularly pro-Basque . . . but I'm Basque first and then Spanish, but it depends where I am.'

Nacho's hierarchy clearly relates to identity in the same way that Marc's discussion of home is about more than locating somewhere on a map. Again, as with the discussion of multiple homes, the possibility of competing, or at least differing identities, was not something that respondents found difficult but, on the contrary, was often a subject that they enjoyed talking about and the question often stimulated a conversation with themselves as much with the interviewer. This very much gives us a sense of how the concepts of home and belonging are constructed, in our case through narrative, rather than something that is given.

Meanings of home

Our discussion of where is home, and identities attached to this, is closely linked to an understanding of meanings of home. The subject of meanings of home is important in philosophical and psychological writings on place and identity. One of the best known accounts is Bachelard's (1964) philosophy of space, which is based on an exploration of poetic images of home. Bachelard's intention is to move beyond mere descriptions of home (or 'house' as it is translated from the French) to 'isolate, an intimate, concrete essence that would be a justification of the uncommon value of all of our images of protected intimacy' (Bachelard 1964: 3). His account of home/house is therefore of an essentialist emotional attachment to any space that gives shelter, or this sense of 'home'. Yet while recognizing the plurality of homes, Bachelard (1964: 7) has particular affection for childhood homes in creating a sense of being in the world, as 'the environment in which the protective beings live'. We never truly leave this home but frequently revisit it in our daydreams.

Closely influenced by phenomenological writings on home, environmental psychologists have examined emotional attachments to and meanings of home. Many of these studies build uncritically on the phenomenological approach, to explore the meanings of home through empirical research (Hayward, 1975; Sixsmith, 1986; Després, 1991). One important perspective of empirical inquiry is how meanings of home are structured by life-course events, hence temporal aspects of home are addressed (Werner et al., 1985), although this has tended to develop a very individualized account of variation

(Somerville, 1997). What emerge from this approach are comprehensive lists of meanings of home, illustrating the richness and complexity of emotions that individuals associate with home (Moore, 2000). Yet this list-generating approach to meanings of home also accentuates the sense of universality of home. Possible sources of variation in meanings associated with home have been explored for particular groups, including young people (Keynon, 1999; Rosh White, 2002), the elderly (Sixsmith and Sixsmith, 1991; Hockey, 1999), the homeless (Somerville, 1992; Kellett and Moore, 2003), and ethnic groups (Fog Olwig, 1999). This focus on these particular groups has resulted in a reduced accentuation of the positive and more emphasis on generating a critical perspective, particularly from a feminist approach (Hunt, 1989; Madigan et al., 1990; Gurney, 1997). Cross-national studies of homes have tended, in the most part, to focus on material structures and housing design, including universal features of spatial aspects of home (Altman and Gauvin, 1981); culturally embodied meanings of built environments (Rapoport, 1969) and the relationship between housing and family forms (Birdwell-Pheasant and Lawrence-Zúniga, 1999).

What is of particular interest to us is the extent to which it is possible to generalize about home across different contexts. Accounts that take as their starting point a Bachelardian view of the eternal essence of home look towards an essential poetry of space that transcends context. Yet this romantic view of home is one that is repeatedly challenged as inappropriate, particularly for women, ethnic groups and young people and children. Moreover, as outlined in Chapter 2, we are particularly interested in the spatial practices of home and do not see home as something that is given. There is a tension here between recognizing the fundamental importance of having a home and belonging, but also how this is actually realized in everyday lives in different contexts, that suggests that home will not necessarily have the same universal meaning.

We have sought to develop a theoretical perspective of home that is both sensitive to the depth of meanings associated with home and the relational aspects of home, which can in turn provide a framework to explore the potential conflict between the apparent universality of emotional attachments to home and the varied lived experiences. We agree with Somerville (1997) that while a sociological approach that emphasizes relational aspects of home and/ or an anthropological one that explores the material context of home both offer an alternative to phenomenological interpretations of meanings, none of these perspectives on their own effectively deal with the complexity of home. Somerville makes the case for a multi-disciplinary approach to home by adopting a social phenomenological framework that looks at 'domestic relations as entirely constituted by experience and action, and vice versa, domestic experience and action will be viewed as issuing from the material and social realities of domestic structures' (Somerville, 1997: 237). However, while agreeing with Somerville's call for a dialectic understanding, we argue that it is not only material and social realities that frame the experiences and practices of home but that ideological and symbolic meanings need to be incorporated into our theoretical framework. In developing our theoretical perspective of home in this way we have been influenced by Lefebvre's (1991) writing on *The Production of Space*. Lefebvre's influence on contemporary writings about space is undeniable (Shields, 1999; Merrifield, 2000), and in a similar way to which his writings have been used by others (especially Harvey, 1989), we are particularly influenced by the way in which he attempts to combine the more materialist understanding of space with more symbolic or ideological understandings.

The core of Lefebvre's contribution lies in a threefold distinction of space, although in his writings he uses a number of different classifications (Harvey, 1989: 220–1; Merrifield, 2000). A core distinction is between 'spatial practices' (perceived or material space), 'representations of space' (conceived space) and 'representational spaces' (lived space) (Lefebvre, 1991: 33 and 39). Yet there is some ambiguity in how this threefold distinction may be applied empirically. In particular, as Allen and Pryke (1994: 454) argue, the treatment of spatial practices as perceived space is problematic empirically as it implies an artificial distinction between these and lived spaces (that there is an objectified material or 'natural' space that we perceive around us). When thinking about home, this treatment of spatial practices as perceived space is particularly problematic, as Fortier (2003: 127) writes: 'the familial home is a space that is always in construction, not only in the imagination, but in the embodied material and affective labour of women and men.' It is, therefore, difficult to think of what perceived home spaces might refer to as home is essentiality the product of its inhabitants' own labour. In adopting a classification of home spaces we turn to another trinity adopted by Lefebvre when writing about the spectacle of Venice, which he argues generates a unity through 'combin[ing] the city's reality with its ideality, embracing the practical, the symbolic and the imaginary' (Lefebvre, 1991: 74). We have opted for this set of distinctions as the one that relates more clearly to our data on home spaces.

In referring to 'the practical' we are concentrating upon the more material, in the broadest sense of the word, aspects of domestic space. This would include all aspects of buying or renting or otherwise occupying domestic space together with such matters as furnishing, repairing or rebuilding and decorating. With the 'symbolic' we are referring to discourses about and representations of home and domestic space. For the 'imaginary' we unpack how individual meanings are inscribed into domestic space, the relationships between home and personal identity and the linkages between domestic space and autobiography. These three elements can be seen as interacting with and impinging on each other in a triangular relationship.

Each aspect of the trinity of spaces also suggests different approaches to unpacking variation in meanings of home. By exploring the practical home we can compare the material aspects of home, in our case through contrasting different patterns of leaving home and processes surrounding setting up home for the first time. Symbolic discourses about home will be highly contextualized and potentially provide a fruitful approach to identifying variation. Finally with the imaginary we might come closer to a concept of the universal home.

The practical

The practicalities of home making, the production and reproduction of domestic space, were very much to the fore in our accounts. Marte, who is one of the youngest respondents and still living with parents [T 18 F LWP], presents one version of home making that very much recognizes the importance of starting from new:

> I have this feeling that if you build a house by yourself, then it's truly yours . . . if there has been someone living there before you, then it sort of isn't your real home I feel . . . if you are living in an apartment and paying rent, then it becomes your home, but this also has been someone else's home before . . .

While most respondents did not emphasize the idea of building a home from scratch, the possibility of ownership of property was highly endorsed and there was fairly widespread agreement that paying rent was pouring money down the drain (see also Richards, 1990: 120). Whether buying or renting, the most common experience was to move into some existing space that had been home for a previous occupant. The practical work of 'creating a home', is strongly associated with ownership and home improvements, even among young people who have not yet begun this process: 'When you buy your own place and start fitting it out, then I hope and believe this place will be my home' [Katrine T 25 F LWP].

Despite the fact that fewer young people in Britain and Norway leave home to buy a house, compared with their Spanish peers, the association between ownership and appropriation of home through DIY were just as relevant in Liverpool and Trondheim. In fact we found in Bilbao less talk of practical home making as the notion of *casa* tended to refer to existing or given space that is transformed through family living into a *hogar*. This can be linked to the greater tendency to leave home to get married in Spain and the clearer overlap between family and *hogar*, as Julia who has left home and is living with her partner describes: 'we're in the process of creating a partnership, and creating a *hogar*; we're in process of doing both things, no?' [Julia B 29 F LH].

One exception here is where Spanish young people moved into a 'family' house that had previously belonged to uncles/aunts, grandparents, or in-laws. Here the process of practical home making did take on added meaning and significance, as María, who moved to a house in the same compound as her in-laws, describes: 'I feel that it is their [parents-in-law] house, not mine. But as it is decorated, more of my things are here, I feel like . . . the four walls are not mine but the space inside is my own' [María B 27 F LH].

All our respondents were very much aware of the costs of housing and a range of procedures was adopted to assist the new homemakers. These included various forms of family assistance, for example help towards a deposit, contribution to mortgage interest payments, even gifts of houses (Holdsworth, 2004). These practicalities also extended beyond the provision of financial support to assistance in the process of moving and in furnishing the new home.

The symbolic

Discussions of the symbolic home emerged less directly than practical issues, but through the exchanges between researcher and respondent, often in the repetition of some fairly well-known phrases. Liverpool respondents would refer to 'a house is not a home' or 'home is where the heart is'. In the Trondheim interviews we were told on more than one occasion that home is 'more than just a place to sleep'.

Respondents also talked about the importance of 'everyone' needing a home. Yet in the Basque country *casa* may take on added significance as a symbol of Basque identity. The Basque house, or *Baserria*, is an essential part of the Basque landscape, although the actual experience of living in a *Baserria* may be more of a myth than an actual reality (Douglass, 1988). A couple of respondents explicitly made the link between *casa* and cultural heritage. One father talked about *casa* representing his family and ancestors. Other respondents talked about *casa* as their *pueblo*. Hence, while initially we might find considerable universality in the symbolism of home, the material aspects of the symbolic home are very much culturally embedded and serve as an important marker of cultural, or regional, identity.

Another way of integrating the symbolism of home is through the experiences of young people who had traumatic home lives, many of whom ended up leaving abruptly. We found that rather than associating home with negative emotions, these young people tended to define themselves as 'homeless', as the symbolism of home did not correspond to their experiences. We discussed Sharon's and Helen's difficult departures briefly in the preceding chapter, and they are relevant here. Sharon [21, LH, L] appears to have no sense of home whatsoever; home is just a place to live. Helen [17, LH, L] defined herself as homeless and looked back, with some distress, to a home with her mother and sister, when she was happy. Laia [29, LAH, B], unlike Helen and Sharon, still lives at home but she does not see where she lives as her home: Rather, it is her parent's home and she concludes that she does not have a home. For these three, therefore, home is possibly elsewhere in the past or the future but it is not where they are living at present.

The imaginary

A classic statement of the imaginary in domestic space was provided by Seeley et al. (1956: 43) in their Crestwood Heights study: 'the home is . . . much more than a repository of artefacts; it is in its own right and *par excellence* an artefact to which deeply buried meanings are attached'. Our interview material is very rich with these accounts, especially for young people who were in the process of leaving home or who had not yet left, and for whom the imagined home formed part of what they were working to create, as Nina, who is living at home, describes:

> Because if I was to go into my own home, I'd have to create a home, you know, with my own things there. That would also be somewhere where I had, you know, where I could relax and be myself, you know, even should I be on my own. [Nina L 25 F LWP]

Yet the imagined home is also a powerful image for those who have experienced different homes. Odd [T 26 M LH] conveys the sense of the imagined home and the way in which meanings are created when he says:

> It must be a place that gives you a happy feeling . . . Imagine that you have been away for sometime, maybe travelling somewhere, and when you return you get a feeling of fulfilment, of being very relaxed and happy to be home, if you know what I mean . . . Something that you can identify with is waiting for you on your return . . . that is important for me . . .

The imaginary home therefore allows individuals to combine practical and symbolic homes but can also stand in opposition to these. For respondents without a clear sense of the practical home, for example young people who had not left, or whose experiences did not accord with symbolic ideals, the imaginary is an important alternative to their lived experiences. This use of the imaginary in this way tends to be more prominent among young people than parents, but not necessarily. One young respondent from Liverpool talked about her father's desire to move to Devon following his divorce, where he thought he would find a spiritual home.

Utopian homes

In analysing both the symbolic and the imaginary home it is impossible to ignore their utopian element, which varies little by country, residential status or age. We could almost illustrate the utopian from any of the interviews and it would be difficult to identify the respondent's location, age or gender, as the following selection illustrate:

> A place where I do feel secure and feel extremely comfortable. [Nina L]

> Somewhere where you feel safe and secured and loved and cared for. [Mother L]

> Something stable . . . a place in which you feel cut-off from the world. [Peru B]

> Family, seclusion, protection, security and intimacy. [Father B]

> That means a safe and secure place. [Espen T]

> A place where I feel comfortable and that I belong to . . . [Andrea T]

> I believe it important to be able to return to a home that enables me to feel safe. You feel that at least there you are able to be your true self, arranging it the way you like. I think this is closely related to feeling secure, having a good home means security . . . for me this is important . . . [Katrine T]

Some stress the idea of a place where you can 'be yourself', whereas others emphasize the links with family. But the most popular themes are the linked ideas of security, peace, safety, comfort and warmth, with security as the core idea. These were living endorsements of the title of Lasch's book, *Haven in a Heartless World* or of Bachelard's (1964) writings on the poetic landscapes of home. These terms all refer to both psychological states and physical or embodied conditions, modes of being in the world. What is interesting, apart from the sheer ubiquity of these responses, is that the reader has little sense of what the home is secure against. This echoes Massey's (1992) observation about the paradox of treating home as a bounded space, yet at the same time home cannot be reduced to a fixed space, its very essence is that it takes different forms over time and space. For example, Katrine's reference to returning to a home in particular suggests a simple inside/outside distinction without indicating anything about the actual outside.

What, then, is utopian about these accounts? The relatively high level of abstraction linked to a strong personal identification with this idea suggests, as Lefebvre argues, a convergence of the symbolic and the imaginary, hence it is often difficult to distinguish between the two. It is probable that our respondents were aware of the darker sides of family and domestic life, whether one is talking about violence and abuse, conflicts and tensions or accidents in the home. Indeed some of our respondents had personal experiences of violence and conflict. Certainly we had little, if any, signs of 'dystopic' visions of the home of the kind indicated by Douglas (1991: 287) that 'the more we reflect on the tyranny of the home, the less surprising it is that the young work to be free of its scrutiny and control'. Young people and parents alike were united in their recognition of the utopian home. Many young people were aware of the tyrannies (although few would use such a strong term) of the home, but this does not necessarily mean that they are more likely to break out and seek some alternative mode of living. Some young people did talk about their aspirations for 'alternative' homes, such as living on boat (see discussion of Peru's narrative below), or by the sea, yet none had realized these projects. For most young people whom we interviewed it is almost as if they wish to set up their own 'tyrannies' when they themselves begin to have children. Similarly, Sibley (1995: 129) writes 'much of the literature on the home . . . fails to convey the frustrations and anxieties that may be associated with home life.' We would broadly agree with this characterization of much of the literature but would argue that this process of 'editing out' is also found in our more everyday accounts, and much of the empirical data on home 'have a Bachelardian ring to them' (Korosec-Serfaty, 1995: 272). There may be a middle-class bias in many scholarly discussions of the idea of home (Després, 1991) but such a bias is not confined to scholars.

Case studies

In order to illustrate the inter-relations between these three different ways of conceptualizing home we discuss the case studies of two young people in more detail, both of whom have very different experiences and expectations of home.

Peru is a middle-class student, 24 years old, who lives at home with his parents in Bilbao. He describes himself as very idealistic and strong willed, and throughout his interview talked a lot about the conflicts that he has had with his parents. He is therefore atypical in a Spanish sense in that he sees himself doing his own thing and not what his parents want him to do. Despite this he still lives at home as he recognizes the advantages that it gives him in terms of saving money, because he is at the moment saving up for a trip to India. He rejects the idea of settling down and becoming rooted in one place, again something that stands out in the Bilbao context, where most of the other respondents expressed a desire to stay local. His narrative is therefore full of contradictions between a desire to be different and a free spirit with the fact that he has not actually achieved his goal of travelling and is still living at home.

Peru talked a lot about what home means to him, in particular what his ideal of home is:

Interviewer: What does the idea of *casa* mean to you?
Peru: *Casa?* . . . well *casa* means something stable, doesn't it? A *casa*, a *hogar*. And at the moment I don't have the need to have anything stable. *Casa* also signifies a place where you can shut out the rest of the world and in which you feel . . . it's your land, your place but I don't have this sensation to need my own demarcated place. I love camping; for me my place is to go to the beach and have open spaces, you understand? . . . I don't need . . . I don't know . . . to have 40, 50 metres to adorn with things and to make it pretty . . .

Peru's ideal of *casa* rejects the more usual symbolic notions of home as a place of security and sanctuary. His imaginary home is therefore one that is formed in opposition to the symbolic concepts of a demarcated and bounded space. He also rejects the ideal of ownership, instead preferring to embrace home as a temporal and open space.

When it comes to identifying where home is, Peru recognizes that his parents' house is his *casa* in the sense that he has always lived there, but that ultimately it is his parents' house,

Interviewer: Do you consider here to be YOUR home?
Peru: No, this *casa* is my parents' and its where I live. And I like it here more or less, but it's not my *casa*, it's not my *casa* because . . . well . . . yes it's my *casa*. You see it depends on your point of view. It is my *casa* because I have always lived here and I feel that I come here, I enter here and it is my *casa*. But it is not my *casa*, it's not my *hogar*, it's my parents' *hogar* and I like it, eh? Above all now, because we have had difficult times and ultimately I like it.

In trying to explain his confusion, Peru suggests that ultimately it is not his *casa*, as he as not created it as is own. As his ideal is not a fixed place, his parents' house can never fulfil his imaginary ideal of home:

Yes, that it doesn't mean that . . . I have not created my own *casa*. But it's not that I don't have an idea of what *casa* is, as I have already told you, as something . . . I could quite happily live on a boat and I really like that idea . . . a *casa* that moves. I love this idea of a snail. I like that a lot. Now if I go away on a trip, if I go to India on a bike and I take my tent well, it could be . . .

For Peru, therefore, his strong sense of the imaginary home stands in opposition to both symbolic and material forms of home (the latter referring to where he actually lives). Meanings of home for Peru therefore provide a way of resisting what is expected of him and provide an ideal to which he can at least aspire and that he hopes to realize.

Lisa is from Liverpool and is 25. She comes from a working-class background and is currently doing voluntary work while looking after her son. She first left home when she was 18 to live with her boyfriend, although her parents did not approve. Lisa describes in a moving and very painful account how her boyfriend's behaviour became increasingly aggressive towards her, particularly after she fell pregnant. Over the course of a few months, her boyfriend repeatedly beat her if she threatened to leave. When she did try to escape he attempted to set fire to the flat. In the end Lisa jumped out of a first-floor window to escape. She broke down when she got to her Mum's when she finally admitted what had been happening. Lisa describes how her mother was so upset that Lisa had not confided in her parents earlier. Her reason for not doing so at the time was in part because she did not want to admit to her parents that they had been right about her moving out:

'Cos I thought I was so great when I first left. I was bragging about how good I was doing. And then for such a short time later, for everything to go completely wrong, like me whole world collapse, and not only that, I found out I was pregnant as well, it was absolutely horrendous. The last thing I wanted to do was go and see me mum and dad. And yet in another sense, the first thing I wanted to do was come home. You know, it was just, to be looked after; for someone to care about me again. I'd been alone for so long. It was awful.

Lisa clearly sees going back to her parents as returning home, that the abuse and isolation she had suffered when living with her boyfriend meant that returning to her parents felt like going 'home'. Later on she got back together briefly with her boyfriend, although this did not work out and Lisa could not bring herself to leave 'home', her parents' house, again. Lisa has since married a new partner and left home for the second time, although her sense of home is still strongly associated with her parents' home as a place of love and warmth:

Lisa: Because I felt happy and safe here [parents' home]. And I knew I was genuinely loved and cared about here. And I still feel safe here now;

I'm happy, I still consider this, even though I've got me own house and me husband and me children, this is still me home. It's weird.

Interviewer: As you say, its where you feel safe – its where you've been looked after and you've been loved.

Lisa: Yeah. I was here for so long; its just, its just great, you know, completely home. Its wonderful. And I have to say, even now, when I go home, you know I'm worrying about what I've got to clean, what needs ironing, what needs washing. I come here and I've got none of that.

For Lisa the overwhelming positive feelings that she has for her parents' home are clearly associated with her experiences when she first left home and are more important than the practical side of her married home. Lisa's account would clearly fit a Bachelardian view of the positive emotional quality of childhood homes. Moreover, she feels the weight of having to do things in her new home in a negative way. This clearly relates to feminist critiques of emotional ideals of home that ignore the fact that home is a place of work for women, as much as a site for love and leisure (Hunt, 1989). However, when reflecting on what home means to her, Lisa talks very positively about where she lives and endorses the symbolic view of home as a place of safety:

Its, I don't know, I just feel better when I'm at home, I always look forward to going home when I've been out. I just like being there; it makes me feel safe and secure. Relaxed. That's why I associate all that with home. You know, that feeling of safeness and security and the, you know, when I get through the front door, after having a hard day when I've been out with the kids or shopping, or whatever, its, yeah it is, it's like a great sense of relief to be in there. Just to be home. I love the space! (laughs). 'Cos I do, I love me house, I know its mine. You know, no one can take it away from me.

Lisa's account is particularly interesting, not just because it reflects so much of what widely held believes about what home should be like, but that despite what happened to her when she first left, or maybe because of what happened, her recognition of home as a place of safety and security is so strong.

Creating a home

As we have explained, 'home' cannot be taken either as referring to a unique spatial location or as having a unique meaning. This sense of multiple homes is, for most people, compatible with the fact that they have a place to call home, be it a room in a house, a family home, or their 'own' home. Yet home is not, ideally, a given space but one that is created through emotional and practical work. The importance of creating a home is clearly evident in the discussions of the practical home. In the UK for example the popularity of home-makeover television programmes is an illustration of the modern *zeitgeist*, that it is not sufficient to own a home but that it should be decorated and stylized in accordance with contemporary fashions.

Yet there are different ways that we might go about this project, in particular Lefebvre when writing about producing space, distinguishes between dominated and appropriate spaces that are relevant in understanding the process of home making. Lefebvre (1991: 337) argues that dominated space was fostered by capitalism through the dominance of exchange values over use values and the buying or renting of 'volumes of space' instead of land. Yet, as space assumes a more important role in modern societies, and the mode of production of space comes to the fore, this, he argues, 'implies a shift from domination to appropriation' (Lefebvre 1991: 410). Moreover, the process of appropriation of space does not just refer to specific home spaces but to 'their meanings and the modes of relationships one establishes with them' (Korosec-Serfaty, 1985: 76).

Despite the current vogue for instant makeover television programmes, a common theme throughout the interviews is the idea that a home is something to be worked out, that it is not an instantaneous creation, reflecting Lefebvre's argument that we are 'inspired to *appropriate* rather than dominate space' (Blum and Nast, 1996: 575). Indeed, we could say that the theme of appropriating space was a core narrative in the leaving-home process. However, it begins within the parental home and our accounts are full of descriptions of 'rooms of one's own' within the parental home and the ways in which these are transformed into personalized living spaces through possessions, relative freedom of access and the possibilities of entertaining friends. With the accounts of 'home-making' this sense of appropriating space becomes even more apparent. Home is not just 'given' space. Saile (1985) refers to 'the ritual establishment of home'; and we would support this phrase seeing ritual in its fullest, richest range of meanings and the establishment as an ongoing process and not a once-and-for-all accomplishment. Appropriation takes on a material dimension, with many references to DIY and ownership, yet the transformation of 'houses into homes' is also associated with emotional work, particularly though the project of family formation. Unlike the more material aspects of home making, emotional work is often more timeless and open-ended, a project that is 'never complete' (although doubtless there are many DIY enthusiasts who may echo this!).

Discussions of dominating and appropriating spaces assume that the individual concerned is in a position to reproduce space in this way. However, experiences of home do not always allow for individual agency. Another aspect of domination is how domestic space can become dominating both across the life-course and for different family members (Fortier, 2003). As Miller (2002: 4) observes when thinking about agency and home, this does not just entail what we do to homes, but 'what the home does to us'. For example, the Englishman's castle may be a prison to the Englishman's wife, son or daughter. We can, therefore, think about the ways in which domestic space can be seem to dominate or overwhelm individuals and as such limit their capacities to shape and appropriate space in terms of their own personal or shared projects.

Respondents both old and young, especially women, referred to the experience of being dominated by space. In most cases these referred to sur-veillance in the parental home, mainly by parents of young women, but also by male members of the household of women regardless of age. Yet unease at home is not something that is restricted to young people living with parents, or partners. Olivia, a young Spanish women who has left home to live with friends following an argument with her father, reflected on a sense on unease in her new *casa*:

> This *casa* is my place but I'm not very comfortable here . . . It is the *casa* that I don't like much, not that it isn't my parents' *casa*. It is more because of the *casa*. In my room, for example, I'm happy. In the living room, if I'm there for a couple of hours, it oppresses me. I come here and I'm uncomfortable. [Olivia B 23 F LH]

Experiences of being dominated by space are often linked to young people's sense of alienation and inability to change the space that they occupy.

Concluding remarks

We began this chapter by looking at how respondents dealt with questions about where/what is home, which initially, we proposed, could elucidate important cultural variation in identifying home that were related to linguistic differences. Yet while there is clearly a distinction in how respond-ents in Bilbao initially dealt with the questions on *casa*, essentially we find considerable similarity in how young people and parents warmed to the sub-ject of home. And warm they did, which at least initially appears to be strong endorsement of a Bacheladian approach, that we can distil an essential emo-tional quality of home that transcends context. However, while a sense of the 'utopian' home does emerge, it is only giving us a partial take of the full experiences of home. Our trinity of home spaces does produce a more diverse account of home than merely concentrating on the more symbolic and given meanings. Instead, both the practical dimensions reflect cultural differences in housing design and build as well as practices of leaving home, while imagery homes are more personally situated accounts and images.

We find that images and ideals of home are as important as, if not more important, than actual lived experiences in generating a sense of home. We need to distinguish between the construction of a home and the construction of the idea of home and the relationships between them. The former is largely to do with the practical construction of space; the latter with the interplays between the imaginary and the symbolic. We also contend the distinction between the symbolic and the imaginary should not be overlooked. The two often do come together but we should not lose sight of how the imaginary allows for individuals to construct their own ideology of home and resist more dominant symbolic readings or practical constructions. Evoking the trinity of practical, symbolic and imaginary homes, therefore allows us to see how personalized meanings and experiences of home may come about, while recognizing how homes, and the relational aspects of home, are produced through shared activities and experiences.

5 Independence

Independence? That's middle class blasphemy. We are all dependent on one another, every soul of us on earth.

(George Bernard Shaw)

If we wanted to identify a defining theme of youth research, then independence would be a reasonable concept to use. So much of what is written about young people is orientated around prospects of achieving independence and, as such, it is a useful way of approaching different perspectives on young people's lives. From a theoretical perspective our understanding of how young people experience transitions to independence has been refreshed by the emerging consensus (using the term loosely) towards more integrated approaches that focus on young people's lived experiences within structural constraints and opportunities. As we discussed in Chapter 2, the theorization of youth that places young people in relation to the dualism between dependence and independence and assumes a linear transition from one to the other, has been challenged both from a theoretical standpoint that recognizes the need to more thoroughly account for forms of agency and lived experiences, and from empirical findings that reveal the complexities of transitions and inter-dependencies. This chapter follows these debates and is structured around the following themes:

- Definitions and different domains of independence: how do young people and parents define independence in respect to different aspects of their lives, such as being economically or emotionally independent, or autonomous?
- How can we conceptualize the relationship between independence and leaving home?
- To what extent are young people's experiences better viewed as shifted forms of inter-dependencies, as Punch (2002) describes, rather than linear transitions from dependence to independence?
- Spatial practices of inter-dependencies and leaving home.

We take as our starting point the observation that a linear dualism of dependence versus independence cannot do justice to the variety of young people's lived experiences, yet we would not want to argue that the notion of the transition is irrelevant (MacDonald et al., 2001). Rather, what we need to consider is not just how transitions are diverging (as in the case of yo-yo transitions, which explicitly recognize the non-linearity of youth transitions, see EGRIS, 2001) but also how the start and end points of youth transitions are not necessarily clearly demarcated states.

What do we mean by independence?

Writing about the 'shame of dependence', Sennett (2003) identifies the stigma of being dependent within the tradition of liberal political philosophy and its concept of adulthood. This ideal is neatly conceptualized by the claim of Senator Patrick Moynihan, an American welfare reformer, that '[dependency] is an incomplete state in life: normal in the child, abnormal in the adult' (Sennett, 2003: 102). In the classic texts of liberal thought, from Locke to Mill, the recognition of the capacity to act rationally and make one's own judgements, is what divides a child from an adult, and as such it is the duty of the state to facilitate young people to become independent adults. Our desire and need to be independent is inextricably linked to the values of freedom and liberty, which as Berlin (2002: 168) writes '[l]ike happiness and goodness, like nature and reality [freedom] is a term whose meaning is so porous that there is little interpretation that it seems able to resist'. The benefits of freedom and liberty are seemingly so overwhelming that they do not need to be defended. Yet, as we shall explore in this chapter, the moral pre-eminence of independence is not something that we should, or necessarily do, take for granted.

A good starting point in trying to define independence is, therefore, to consider the various forms that it might take. Classic liberal thought provides a useful starting point. Writers on the idea of freedom, such as Berlin, frequently distinguish between a negative and a positive idea of freedom, the first being freedom from certain kinds of constraints or controls, the latter referring to a freedom to do certain things or to be a certain kind of person. While Berlin acknowledges that the distinction can sound quite false, in that the two are a negative and positive way of stating the same thing, he famously claims that the difference between them is not trivial, and that the questions 'who is master?' and 'over what area am I master?' demand very different responses (Berlin, 2002: 36). These kinds of polarizations could certainly be applied to ideas of independence. In particular, it maps quite closely to a northern/southern spilt in our interview material. In Norway and Britain there is a greater tendency to view independence as being free from parental constraints, while in Spain we find greater emphasis on the positive aspects of freedom, with many Spanish young people arguing that living in the parental home is not necessarily identified with restrictions. Indeed, parents and young people both recognize that younger generations are given the opportunity to be free within the parental home 'to be' what they want to be, hence they have their independence. Take, for example, the mother of one of the Spanish interviewees [son aged 28, LWP]:

> I think that [name] is independent living here because he does what he wants to do: you see, I have never . . . I do not put upon him any kind of problems about being here more, neither do I not see him, it is, I do not give him any conditions, it is, he is here, he comes to sleep but he is independent, for, well because he has his own life.

It would seem that both parents and young people in Bilbao are able to adapt to prolonged stays in the parental home by allowing for young people to have this autonomy within the parental home. Though to a certain extent the degree to which young people and parents are able to facilitate this will depend on other factors, particularly spatial and economic constraints, which in turn will be closely inter-connected. For example, Pepi is 28 and lives at home with her parents. Her father is a doctor, there is little evidence of financial constraints at home, and Pepi has her own sitting room and bedroom. She has considerable space at home to be 'independent'. While Pepi's living arrangements are not typical, other young people associate being independent with going out and, as such, using space outside of the home is important. We might reflect that the climate is Spain will play a role in facilitating this spatial freedom. Yet where spatial and financial resources are tight, it is much harder for both parents and adult children to achieve independence while living together. For example, Maite is a mother with four adult children. She works as a cleaner and her husband has retired due to ill-health. Maite viewed her children's departure as beneficial because it was both expensive and labour-intensive for her while they lived at home, although she recognizes that other parents would not see it this way:

> Yes it hurts them [parents in general] when their children leave. For some it's because their children are best [living at home] . . . and I say 'but also it's good my way'. I want them to become independent; and that also when they lived in my house they did things that I didn't like.

Experiences of independence within the parental home are not absent in the British and Norwegian interviews although a sense of the constraints of family life seem to emerge much more strongly. Jane is a student at university, and her experiences represent a very stark contrast to her Spanish peers. Like Pepi she comes from a wealthy family (her father is a banker) but, unlike Pepi, she does not live with her parents and has no expectation of living with them again. In fact she has not spent much time living with her parents since she was 13, when she went to boarding school. Her parents now live abroad and have bought a flat in London for her and her brother for when they are not at university. Jane's experience of being independent is, therefore, defined by not being subject to her parents' authority: 'I don't think I'd like it, though, to come back from university where I've been completely independent and have to go in, back to someone else's rules' [Jane L 20 F LH].

While Jane's experiences of going to boarding school and having her own independent life at university and in her flat in London are facilitated by her class background, other young people in Britain and Norway from very different backgrounds echo her sentiments about being free from parents. Sharon lives in Liverpool. From the age of 14 months to 17 years she lived with foster parents. At 17 she was eligible for a leaving care grant and felt that she did not need her foster parents' support anymore so she left, living first in a young-person's housing project before moving into a local authority flat. She now works as a care assistant. Though her background is clearly very different from Jane's, her sense of independence is similar:

> Interviewer: Yeah. And what would you say being independent means for you?
> Sharon: Your own space.
> Interviewer: Yeah. Anything else? . . .
> Sharon: Your own life; you can do what you want. You don't have people telling you what to do.

Domains of independence

Another approach to defining what we mean by independence is to recognize the different spheres to which it pertains. Independence is often associated with economic criteria, not least as this form is easier to define and measure. Proxies for economic independence include having a secure and sufficient income, ability to pay for housing and lack of reliance on welfare support, as well as less direct measures relating to consumption (Jones and Wallace, 1992). Other aspects of young people's lives may be reduced to economic criteria, for example young people's dependence on parents is usually identified as financial reliance on parents, rather than other relational characteristics (see, for example, Schneider, 2000). The ability to be able to support one's self financially may also be taken as a necessary condition for other forms of freedom, as Jones and Wallace (1992: 154) describe:

the imposition of dependency status on many young people who in other historical and social circumstances might be able to live independent lives, takes away adult responsibility and places young people under the legal control of their parents. Their rights to freedom and self-determination are thus restricted.

Here economic independence is taken as the guarantee of personal freedom, with other dependent relations that young people experience determined by their inability to achieve economic independence.

It is important, however, to contextualize this dominance of economic criteria, as it reflects the problems facing young people in achieving economic independence. The most significant impacts on young people's lives in Great Britain since the 1970s have been the collapse of the youth labour market, extension of education and training, and withdrawal of state benefits (Hutson and Jenkins, 1989; Allatt and Yeandle, 1992). These concerns are echoed elsewhere in Europe and North America. The structural determinants vary, particularly regarding welfare provision for young people, but the pattern of withdrawal of employment options and extension of training/education is replicated in many different contexts (see for example, Roberts et al., 2002).

Yet independence is not just a characteristic of economic relations, but pertains to emotional, psychological and political ones as well. These are defined in various ways including the capacity to support oneself financially, not rely on others, take care of oneself, and to think and act without interference from others. Fraser and Gordon (1994) define four meanings of independence: economic, moral/psychological, socio-legal and political. They argue that the relationships between the different dimensions are not clear, and there are no necessary causal connections between them.

Associations between the different dimensions are often inter-dependent. For example, there may often be complex and fluid relationships between economic and moral or psychological dependencies.

In our data we find less emphasis on socio-legal or political dimensions but there is a lot of discussion about independence in terms of economic and emotional criteria. This also includes more psychological distinctions that understand independence in terms of a sense of autonomy. These criteria, as we explore throughout the chapter are rarely used as distinct entities. If we take economic independence, very few of our respondents use it in the same way that Jones and Wallace do, in that it is not earning an income that defines independence, but taking responsibility for financial matters, such as paying bills and not getting into debt (this though is quite common, particularly among Liverpool respondents). Being economically independent is recognized as being responsible about money, rather than how much money young people actually have. The exceptions are young people such as José, who is unemployed and living with his parents in Bilbao and whose account we describe below. He clearly associates his lack of independence with his lack of funds.

Rejecting the ideal that independence can be neatly encapsulated by economic criteria does not necessarily mean that we are dismissing the struggles that people achieve in order to become independent, but that it is important to reflect on how young people negotiate both independence and dependency. Contextualizing independence is key; debates about youth and economic independence heightened at a time when it was objectively harder for young people to establish this, and the dominance of the economic model in youth transitions studies was influenced by contracting opportunities for young people. However, we should also note that the recognition of economic hardship was taken up by the early pioneers of cultural youth studies, with very different research outcomes, in that the overall drive of the influential work carried out at the Centre for Contemporary Cultural Studies (see, for example, Hall and Jefferson, 1977) was towards ethnographic studies of youth sub-cultures and practices of resistance. Both approaches recognize the structural barriers facing young people, with one approach directed towards how young people might go about achieving the end goal of economic independence, and the other towards how this was associated with sub-culture formation and resistance to state policy and unemployment.

Independence and leaving home

Conventionally leaving home is taken as an indicator of independence: 'independence is symbolized by leaving home and setting up an independent household' (Allatt and Yeandle, 1992: 60). This definition itself raises further ambiguities as to how we might define an 'independent household', but residential transitions are often treated as unproblematic markers of independence. In some studies, establishing a new household is taken as *the* marker of independence (for example, Fernández Córdon, 1997). The flip side of this relationship is that not leaving is regarded as a failure to achieve independence. For example, the research literature on leaving home uses terms such as 'Boomerang Kids' and 'Incompletely Launched Adults', to describe young people who return home after leaving, implying that these broken transitions are 'failures' (Schnaiberg and Goldenberg, 1989; Veevers and Mitchell, 1998). Yet there is very little consideration in the literature as to how the mapping of living with parents/leaving home to dependence/independence works in practice. Descriptive accounts of leaving home patterns throughout modern industrialized societies illustrate the increasingly contradictory nature of young people's lives and housing trajectories, and it is becoming harder to justify the ways in which not leaving home should necessarily be treated as problematic.

Changes in patterns of leaving home both over time and space suggest at least a varying relationship between leaving home and independence. Taking a broad historical perspective, the functional link between leaving home, independence and adulthood emerged as a key characteristic of more modern societies, in contrast to traditional societies where the emphasis was more in terms of shifts of patterns of inter-dependencies, rather than the straightforward achievement of independence (Jones and Wallace, 1992). As employment, education, housing and family transitions converged in modern societies, the functional relationships between these transitions becomes more transparent, and leaving home could be regarded as a signifier of transitions to independence (Jones, 1995). Hence as youth transitions are increasingly being replaced by more fluid and flexible forms, we might expect the link between independence and leaving home to become less transparent. Moreover, if we turn our attention away from North America and north Europe then the functional link between residential independence and 'being independent' is even less appropriate. As we have seen in the discussion of forms of independence, Spanish young people who live at home do not, generally, view themselves as being dependent, but define their independence in different ways to their peers in Britain and Norway. We would expect, therefore, that the experience of leaving home will relate to the different domains of independence in varying ways.

We might expect leaving home to be signifier of economic independence, but in our material residential status is a poor indicator of independence across a range of definitions. Using economic criteria, for example, we find respondents in each location who have well-established jobs but are living at home, while some unemployed respondents or those working in casual/low-paid jobs have left. However the small numbers involved means it is not possible to infer any dominant pattern here; it is more interesting to explore respondents' definitions of independence and how these relate to their own circumstances. Taking economic criteria, most respondents agree that leaving home is an important but not a necessary marker of economic independence. Kristin is 21 and has recently left home in Trondheim. Her comments are consistent with the majority view in all three countries:

> I think that it is more of a grown up thing to be able to own something yourself compared to be living in your parent's house. I think it can be said that you are a more responsible person also when you have your own place . . . I think it is important to be able to financially support yourselves in an independent way, this is an important aspect with becoming an adult I think . . . [Kristin T 21 F LH]

What matters is not how much money someone has *per se* in order to be recognized and to 'feel' independent, but how successfully one manages money and acts in a 'responsible way'.

However, the causal relationship between leaving home and economic independence can be quite subtle. It is more complex than the assumption that young people leave home because they have become financially independent. For example, Adele lives in Liverpool. Prior to leaving home she recognizes that she had a reasonably easy life at home, and that the decision to leave home because she wanted to live with her boyfriend has forced her to become economically independent: 'I think that's another good point about leaving home; I've had to become more financially independent. So, that is another good factor about leaving home . . .' [Adele L 26 F LH].

Leaving home may initiate economic independence for young people for whom lack of employment opportunities in the locale of parents' home is a reason for leaving. José left Bilbao to live in London because he could not find work if he stayed at home. He lived with his girlfriend in London, and found casual employment working in kitchens. On returning to Bilbao after the breakdown of his relationship, he returned to live with his parents. José's account of independence emphasizes the structural constraints that first made him leave, but now make him dependent on his parents once more. He is envious of young people in England, who, he argues, have more opportunities and access to money:

> The English live well . . . Above everything else, they have money, which changes everything. If you can get money you can be economically independent, and well, you can do what you want to do. Everything changes in this way, there is more freedom. And here [in Bilbao] it isn't that there isn't any freedom, it's just that you have to be supervised, in your home. In your parents' house and it's not the same. But no, there [in England] when you want to be able to be independent, you get a flat and you live your own life. [José B 31 M LWP]

José's experiences support the view that independence as a choice is not something that is open to all young people. It is only a choice if you have the opportunity to leave home and find secure employment without relying on welfare. As such we can see that the ideal of being able to leave home because one can support oneself financially outside of the home is determined by class relations, although this does not necessarily mean that young people from less advantaged backgrounds delay leaving home, as lack of employment options and financial constraints can be a reason for leaving, although the extent to which these types of departures are permanent and lead to economic independence is less certain.

For most young people in all three locations leaving home does not necessarily mean that they no longer receive financial support from parents (Holdsworth, 2004). In practice young people, unless they make a deliberate choice never to ask their parents for help, continue to receive various kinds of support after leaving home – for example, financial gifts or loans, or help with moving and DIY. Rather than seeing this as diminishing young people's sense of independence, quite a few respondents recognized that in leaving home they had demonstrated their ability to *cope* on their own, even though they might receive support from others, including partners and parents. We discussed Jane's circumstances earlier on in the chapter. While her parents 'pay' for her to live independently (they bought a flat for her), she stresses the value of being able to cope on her own:

> Well, yes, well, I have grown more independent, obviously from living by myself. Er, but yeah, I think so and also it's the fact that they see me as more independent and they see me as more of an adult now. Because I can cope on my own, you know, do all those things. [Jane, F, 20, LH, L]

As Jane's comment illustrates, it is more important that young people demonstrate the *ability* to act independently and look after themselves financially, than to actually *be* totally independent from parents. Coping is moving beyond purely economic criteria, but is more about personal achievement and recognition by others about taking responsibility.

Valuing independence

Just because an individual has the capacity to be independent, it does not necessarily mean that she is going to act in this way. There are circumstances where independence is not necessarily desired or appropriate. While we might chastise someone for not being able to think for herself, we also recognize the necessity of being able to care for others as the basis of intimacy and personal relations. As Sennett (2003: 119) argues, dismissing the value of asking for help is not necessarily beneficial, either to the individuals concerned or society at large, and the 'fear of asking for help more and more impressed me as a reliable sign of a dysfunctional organization'.

Most young people who we spoke to did recognize themselves as being independent in some way, and recognized a need to be regarded by others as independent (in this case the interviewer) but also to recognize themselves as acting independently. For some young people valuing independence was epitomized by the desire to stand on one's own two feet and not to have to rely on other people. This did not necessarily imply that they would not, from time to time, call on the support of others, what was important was that they do this on their own terms. Both Catherine, who has left home, and Pepi, who is still at home, endorse the idea of being independent in this way:

> . . . I don't like to be dependent, I don't – I like to have people around me that I can call upon, in, when, I need them, or when they need me. But, erm, I don't like being completely dependent on anybody. [Catherine L 26 F LH]

> And well, I generally try to look for ways so that I do not have to depend on people. I do not like to be dependent on people. [Pepi B 28 F LWP]

Being independent is also a 'safety net', not *having* to rely on others is reassuring. When we talked to Chris he had left home two years earlier, in Liverpool, and reflected in some detail on how much being able to stand on his own two feet mattered. He acknowledged the role that his parents played in his life, but for him the fact that he could be independent and survive on his own was very important:

> I've got family, I've got my friends, I've got me job, and I've er, I've got me independence. Right, anything other than that is a bonus. Now they all go hand in hand, really, you know what I mean. Like the job pays for the bills, me mum and dad provide emotional support, and whatever. Now, if I've got anything left over from that, I'll just embrace that and go, 'Yeah, nice one' . . . [Chris L 29 M LH]

Chris goes on to reflect that 'Erm, so, I think its related to independence, really. Its just like, I'm surviving on my own, and I can do things on my own. You know what I mean, so.'

Yet other young people reflect Sennett's observation about the value of seeking out other people, and are more ambivalent towards being 'totally' independent, as Marian, who lives at home with her divorced mother, describes:

> I have always done things alone, always. I don't know . . . then in that sense yes, I consider myself to be independent . . . but on the other hand, me alone, alone-alone-alone, I don't like that. So I always want to seek out someone. [Marian B 20 F LWP]

Most of the respondents who recognized the importance of being with other people are Spanish, not least because, unlike the British and Norwegian young people we interviewed, none of the respondents in Bilbao actually lived alone. Leaving to be alone is relatively unusual in Spain. If young people do not leave home for marriage (by far the most common reason for leaving), then they are more likely to live with either friends or other family members rather than alone. However we might also interpret the fact that none of the Spanish respondents lived alone, and evidence of more willingness to seek out other people, as a culturally informed acceptance that being with and also relying on other people is not necessarily something to be ashamed of.

Inter-dependencies

In recognizing both the different ways that young people might define and value independence, it becomes difficult to demarcate clearly the boundaries between dependence and independence and how leaving home maps onto these. Rather, it is more useful to see young people's experiences as embracing different inter-dependencies, and that these will shift as young people become more independent, particularly around the time of leaving home (and also returning and re-leaving).

Most inter-dependencies involve parents, and to a lesser extent, other family members. As we have seen in the distinction between positive and negative freedom, parents play a crucial role in the way that young people achieve independence, through either facilitating young people to be 'free to' do what they want in their parental home, or conversely, by 'constraining' young people at home. For example, Kjell, from Trondheim, recognizes the role that his parents play in giving him his freedom, though his experience is probably different from those of his peers (although less so from other Spanish young people):

> Yes . . . I would never have stayed at my present place if my parents constantly had invaded my privacy and asked about everything you know . . . Then I would have crashed my head against the wall I think . . . But it might be that other ones of my age think differently so to speak . . . It might be me who has a low threshold so to say, in relation to what I can take actually. It might be that some of my friends who have very involved parents, don't see it the way I see their situation then . . . In regard to my physical surroundings I do feel myself to be independent, yes I do . . . I do get the privacy that I need together with deciding most of my things for myself . . . [Kjell T 25 M LWP]

Taking the opposite view, most British and Norwegian young people endorse Anne Bente's [T 25 F LH] description of the restrictions of living at home:

> Yes . . . the main thing is that they are always able to monitor what you are doing so to speak . . . When you are living on your own you are able for example to watch TV whenever you want to. You do not have to worry about what your parents feel in regards to your actions. It is not that funny to relatively often hear questions like

'aren't you going to do something soon' or 'why are you home at this time, aren't you supposed to be working now or?', and questions like that you know ... And there is also the social aspect you know, because when you are not living on your own, you are always part of something if you know what I mean, when you are home, you are always part of something bigger in a way, part of a family you might say ...

What is apparent in both of these quotations is how relational and spatial processes underpin achieving independence. Kjell talks about independence in terms of his physical surroundings while, in contrast, Anne Bente imagines how physical proximity allows parents to monitor young people's actions. Both refer to relational aspects, although from very different perspectives; Kjell recognizes that his parents are not so involved and therefore give him privacy, whereas Anne Bente recognizes that living at home means being 'part of something bigger', that it entails being with and getting on with others.

For other young people, parents' contribution to their experience of independence is less associated with physical boundaries but is more to do with the ways in which parents may guide them in achieving independence, even if this guidance is not always beneficial. We discuss Joar's experiences of leaving home at a young age in Trondheim in more detail in Chapter 7. Here it is useful to reflect on how Joar recognizes the advice he has been given, in part because he did leave so young (age 16):

Interviewer: What do you think of when I say the word independence?
Joar: Well freedom ... Deciding fully over yourselves also ... This is also something that I've always done, taken my own decisions you know ... But of course, I've been given advice, I must say that ... This advice has probably both been influential sometimes, and sometimes else it hasn't been that influential if you relate it to your prior decisions and actions ... But I have never been forced to do anything actually ... I've been given both good and bad guidance during the years then ... [Joar, M, 27, LH, T]

In fact Anne Bente herself, when thinking about her own relationship with her parents before she left home, also recognizes the active involvement of her parents:

Yes ... one example is education, but they never did say during my teenager-years that I had to be home at for example 10' o clock ... I think they wanted to give me what they called freedom under responsibility. And that resulted in me trying to show them the same trust in return ... so my period at home was positive in that regard ...

In addition to looking at the ways in which parents can encourage young people to become independent, it is also important to consider who is becoming independent from whom. Among our respondents we came across a number of parents and young people who recognized that parents were as dependent on their children for emotional support as children were on their parents. In the majority of cases these were either widowed or divorced women, or mothers whose relationships with their partners were problematic (in one case the father was an alcoholic), and who all had very close relationships with adult daughters (although one widowed mother in Bilbao relied on her son for financial and practical support when he was living at home). In these family units mothers acknowledged how they had become dependent on their daughters for emotional and practical support:

> It has only been us two at all times then . . . so she [her mother] is probably more dependent on me than I am on her, or was I think . . . [Andrea T 28 F LH]

> I think I lean on her too much, I really feel sometimes I'm doing what my Mum did to me and that's in many ways why I would liked her to have gone away [to HE college] because she would have had the space to do her own thing and have her own time [Lydia L P F LWP]

These relationships reflect on how dependency may be gendered within families. Women acknowledge their dependence, reflecting how this is 'normalized' for them. Yet the anxiety expressed by Lydia about how her memory of the relationship she had with her mother influences her daughter's experiences, suggests that the implications of these mother/daughter relationships can be recognized as problematic for younger women. It is also worthwhile to reflect on how these outcomes of close interdependencies between mothers, especially lone mothers, and their daughters are at odds with one of the main findings about leaving home from survey data – that young people who experience their parents' partnership breakdown are more likely to leave home at younger ages. While we only a have a few case studies of these close mother-daughter bonds, which cannot be taken as representative of each country, they do reveal a perspective on growing up with lone parents different from that which dominates popular, but also statistical, discourses. It is also interesting that we find examples of close lone or solo-parenting mother/daughter relationships in all three locations.

Another important form of inter-dependencies is between young people and partners. Leaving might actually entail exchanging one form of dependency for another. This is one form of inter-dependency that we might expect to be gendered, as it is more likely to be women who experience becoming dependent on a partner. In our sample we find a few women who acknowledge this dependency. For example, both Kristin and Adele have left home to live with their partners and recognize that, for them, the transition to 'independence' is less straightforward:

Interviewer: Do you see yourselves as an independent person?
Kristin: Yes I think so . . . but I might not be that, nevertheless I'm dependent on my boyfriend in an economic sense you know, but together me and him form a independent couple if I can say that . . . [Kristin T 21 F LH]

I am glad I've made the move and I've got me own, I wouldn't be without me own flat or house or whatever now, but sometimes I do feel, not trapped, but, that I had more freedom at home than what I have got now [living with her partner]. [Adele L 26 F LH]

Yet, this experience of a new form of 'dependency' is not restricted to women. For example, Joar who is currently unemployed and living with his girlfriend, acknowledges his financial dependency on his partner.

Spatial aspects of independence

Up to now most of our discussion of independence has focused on different ways of conceptualizing and realizing a sense of autonomy as a necessary criteria of independence. Yet it is also important to situate this process, and to think through how independence infers certain spatial parameters and practices.

The importance of privacy is a common theme in defining independence particularly for young people who are living with parents. The aspect of privacy that is important is recognizing someone else's space and not transgressing this – for example, not cleaning a young person's room or not having friends round late. In order for this to work, the rules governing the ways in which individuals maintain their privacy is important. For example, one Bilbao respondent complained about her lack of privacy because her mother would come in when she was lying in bed with a hangover to do the cleaning. One Liverpool respondent had decided to leave home in part because of problems with a younger brother and his lack of awareness of other people's space. These problems are not just restricted to parents and family members but apply to anyone who has the ability to invade one's space. For example, one Liverpool respondent [Lynn L 35 F LWP] described the time that she lived with her boyfriend in her parents' house: 'I was thinking, he's, he's taking away all my space . . . He'd come in, so it is, it's all about space, isn't it, he'd come in to my space, and be taking over my things. And I didn't like it.'

Lynn's account illustrates the importance of recognizing other people's space and the boundaries that define this. While we might, as Sibley (1995) describes, associate a tyrannical household with one where rules are laid down in an authoritarian way and not negotiated, this does not mean to say that the reverse is true and that a totally unregulated home would be any easier to live in. We can, therefore, recognize that the role that parents play in regulating young people's living space may be more positive than that suggested by Anne Bente, whose perception of living at home is very much of being monitored by the parental gaze, which for her is, in the panoptical tradition, potentially all seeing and all knowing.

Marc: a case study

Research on the parenting of older children demonstrates the importance of intimacy at a distance, and the contradictions that parents experience of being close yet at the same time not being too controlling of their children (Jamieson, 1999; Brannen et al., 2000). The management of space and spatial boundaries plays a central role in the way that parents and young people manage inter-dependencies. This can apply to young people living at home as well as for young people who have left. The spatial aspects of leaving home and living with parents do not necessarily infer a linear transition from dependence to independence, but can shed light on how contradictory relations of dependency and independency are managed on a day-to-day basis. For example, one of the few accounts of young people's lives that explicitly deals with these spatial aspects is Leonard's (1980) account of household formation in south Wales, in which she documented how parents use practices of keeping close and spoiling to control their relationships with adult children. In contrast some of our respondents, in all three locations, talked about the ideal of having a certain distance from family members, reflecting as Mason (1999) describes, that you can be too close for comfort to your family. Anna, a mother from Trondheim, reflected that *her* mother had taught her that 'your children ought to live as far away as for you to need a coat to go there'. Space is therefore central to understanding the nuances and contradictions of child/parent relationships prior to, during and after the process of leaving home.

The complexities of the spatial relations of independence emerge in discussions with a number of young people. Marc is 22 and comes from a middle-class background near Liverpool. He left school at age 16 and has had a number of jobs since then. When interviewed he was living at home and working in a local hotel. Marc recognizes that living at home makes him more stubborn about asking for help:

> Interviewer: do you think that [living at home] detracts at all from your sense of independence?
> Marc: Yes, it does, from my own personal sense of independence. It . . .

does in a way, but then it's weird, because I know at any point I can
get out, I can go and drive my car to wherever I want. But then, it
does, because I'll always come back here to – this is my base, so it's
really it's my home . . . But I don't – honest to God, I don't think
about that at all, you know . . .

Interviewer: it is important that you demonstrate that you are capable of
looking after yourself and being independent. Or don't you agree
with that?

Marc: Yes, I suppose I do. Um . . . I don't know whether it's a demonstration or just me being stubborn or . . . it's a bit like a demonstration.
No, it's a demonstration, isn't it? . . . [Marc L 22 M LWP]

Marc therefore recognizes that, because he lives at home, he feels the need
to distance himself from his parents, but that, as the hesitations and repeti-
tions illustrate, it is not something that he feels confident about. In particular,
Marc does not look to his parents for emotional support, yet, as he goes on to
discuss in the interview, the emotional distance that he strives to maintain at
home is not something that he necessarily sees as being intrinsic to his sense of
independence. He recognizes that the way he shuts himself off from other
people, especially his parents, is his way of demonstrating that he is independent, as he finds it harder to establish this by more transparent ways, such as
living independently. He expects, though, that his relationship with his parents will change when he leaves home, in that he may be more willing to chat
to his parents about problems and receive 'help' from them:

If my roles, if the independence swapped, I think I'd be a lot more – I'd
be more – Mum, I've got no money, or . . . You know? Not as bad as
home, more – I've had a horrible day at work, that sort of thing.

But at the moment he maintains an emotional distance from his parents:

Interviewer: Mmm. Do you feel a bit that you're keeping something back
now, because it's kind of like you're trying to have a kind of barrier –
look, this is me, this is you?

Marc: Yes.

Interviewer: But if you had a more physical barrier, i.e. space . . . You were
living outside . . .

Marc: Then I'd ask, I'd let the barrier drop a lot more, yes.

In Marc's account the importance of space is that it determines the kind of
relationship that he has with his parents. While living with his parents he feels
the need to keep something back, partly because he knows it is hard to hide
emotions from people who he sees on a daily basis, echoing Anne Bente's

comments that living at home entails being part of something bigger. Yet if he had a physical barrier between himself and his parents, then he feels he could open up to them more, partly because he can do this on his own terms. Living at home for Marc means that he cannot manage his relationship with his parents in the way that he wants and feels is right for him as an adult. Leaving home and inserting a spatial barrier between himself and his parents will not necessarily mean that he will have less to do with his parents but may actually bring him closer. Marc recognizes that economic independence is a condition for self-esteem and wider notions of independence, although he believes that achieving economic freedom will actually make him more willing to share with others and to have a closer emotional relationship with his parents. This illustrates the inter-dependencies between different dimensions of independence.

We can also use Marc's account to reflect on the relevance of individualization to accounts of dependence, independence and inter-dependencies. Our focus on inter-dependencies would seem initially to be counter-intuitive to the individualization thesis. However, what does emerge from Marc's account, which is similar to those of other young people like him, is the sense that 'it is up to him' and that he has to 'prove himself'. As Bauman (2002: xv) defines it, individualization: 'consists of transforming the human "identity" from a "given" into a "task" – and charging the actors with the responsibility for performing that task and for the consequences of their performance'.

This sense of being charged with the responsibility to prove himself and to remain somewhat aloof from his parents until he achieves this, does reflect the importance Marc places on constructing his own identity, in the way that Bauman describes. We might reflect as to how particular this is to late modern societies, as the moral value of 'proving yourself', often against your background, is not a 'new' ideal.

Concluding remarks

In reassessing the ways in which transitions have been used to analyse young people's lives, we need to reconsider this dualism and the ways it presupposes moralistic treatments of states of dependency and independence. However, we also need to recognize that the precedence associated with achieving independence echoes wider concerns about the potentially disruptive outcomes of dependency, particularly within the context of welfare reform in the US and to a lesser extent in the UK. As Sennett (2003) indicates, the ideology linking dependency and shame is almost hegemonic in these societies. Yet what emerges from an analysis of the interview data is a strong sense of ambiguity surrounding young people's experiences of independence, particularly the ways in which these map on to transitions in employment, education, housing and family formation. At the very least we can see that there is no straightforward sequential relationship between these transitions, and as such there are no necessary stages or processes that young people have to complete to claim to be independent. In fact in some situations the links between various transitions are quite contradictory – for example completing education might involve moving back home and thus equated with a loss of 'independence', or moving in with a partner particularly for women, may, entail moving from one dependent relationship to another. However, while the concept of a goal-orientated transition from dependency to independence is at best a fuzzy ideal for most young people, this did not necessarily mean that independence itself was not valued in some way, although how this is achieved and recognized by others varies considerably.

Relationships between parents and children are key to young people's own evaluation of their independence. If parents allow their children to act in an independent way, in the sense of not laying down rules about comings and goings from the parental home or use of amenities, then young people feel that they have sufficient opportunity to be independent. For other young people, however, their experience of independence while living at home is very much curtailed by the sense of being part of something bigger, and that the opportunities to take control either in terms of their behaviour at home, or even in the sense of the their emotional relationship with parents, are restricted. Leaving home, therefore, may allow young people to have more control over how they interact with parents in time and space. Moreover, in stressing the importance of relationships between parents and children as a key factor in young people's transition to independence, it can be more appropriate to think about inter-dependencies between children and parents. At least for some of the young people who we spoke to, their parents' reliance on them had made it harder for them to leave, or to think about leaving, home.

Relationships with parents and significant others therefore impact on young people's sense of independence and may be regarded as the most important criteria of independence, rather than more tangible attributes (such as having left home, finished education, started work and so forth). Young people's experiences will vary considerably. In particular, the significance of understanding independence through relationships with parents highlights the difficulties facing young people whose relationships with their parents have broken down, or who are leaving care, as they do not have the opportunity of negotiating transitions to independence in this way.

In making sense of the ambiguities and contradictions that emerge from discussions with young people and parents about independence, space is identified as a key factor that impinges on the ways that young people experience independence and/or dependency around the point of departure from the family home. This may relate to practical, symbolic and imaginary forms of home. Within the home space can restrict young people's opportunities for being independent, this is the classic north European approach that prioritizes leaving home as an important prerequisite of independence. Living at home is about being subjected to non-negotiable rules that determine use of space and time. Physical separation can allow a closer relationship between children and parents to emerge, not least because young people are able to manage a more equitable relationship with their parents at a distance. At the very least relationships between parents and young people change during the process of leaving home, yet this does not necessarily mean that young people grow apart from parents – rather, the way they interact changes.

6 Adulthood

Adulthood is the ever-shrinking period between childhood and old age. It is the apparent aim of modern industrial societies to reduce the period to a minimum.

(Thomas Szasz)

Most sociological writing deals with adults, although the sociology of adulthood is relatively under-developed. This paradox has had its parallels in other areas of social enquiry. It is only fairly recently that studies of race and racism have begun to take questions of 'whiteness' seriously and studies of men and masculinity, although now numerous, have only recently emerged in response to the far greater number of studies on women and the challenge of feminist scholarship. In the present example, the contrast is with the sociology of childhood, which is now a flourishing sub-area of social enquiry with numerous journals, conferences and book-length studies. Yet, it is not so long ago that writers in this field were expressing concern about the lack of attention to children and childhood in research and theory (for example, James and Prout, 1997).

There are differences between the studies of race and racism, of gender and of childhood and adulthood but there are also some parallels in the ways in which the studies have developed. In all cases the debate started with recognizing a lack of attention to a particular category (ethnic minorities or race in general, women and gender and, most recently, children). These categories were constructed against another category, which was politically dominant: whites, men and adults. These dominant categories were unexamined because they were part of the taken for granted frame of reference or what Gouldner (1970) called 'domain assumptions'. In a context of structured inequalities it required some effort of imagination, some radical re-framing, to 'see', and to problematize, white people, men and adults. For example, we found one university library catalogue with 1854 references to 'childhood' but only 90 references to 'adulthood'.

In considering the transition out of the parental home, issues of adulthood necessarily come to the fore. This is because, as has already been argued, the move out of the parental home is not simply a change of address but part of a series of other transitions that may or may not be connected: from dependence to independence and from childhood to adulthood. Leaving home is associated with, if not the actual attainment of adulthood, a move in the direction of adulthood. Hence it is important to understand how adulthood is conceived and understood, not only by various professionals or public agencies but also by the social actors themselves as they move into or approach this particular status.

In this chapter we shall consider several overlapping themes:

- Adulthood as an uncertain status. Whether we are talking about public categories or personal understandings, there is a lack of clarity about when adulthood begins and, although to a lesser extent, what it entails.
- Adulthood as a moral category. Adulthood is generally understood in positive terms and as something to do with the moral status of an individual. However, as we shall see, the status of adulthood as a moral category is not always as stable or definite as might at first be supposed.
- Adulthood as a category or frame of understanding which is associated, often in quite complex ways, with other moral categories such as maturity, taking responsibility, independence and so on.
- Adulthood as a category that is negotiated in interactions with significant or generalized others. A sense of adulthood is constructed through numerous encounters and interactions over time, although the effect is not necessarily cumulative.

We shall explore these themes combining some analysis of the relevant literature with more specific studies (including our own) of the leaving-home process.

As an example of the way in which some of these themes are combined, consider the following headline from a newspaper article about Tolkien: 'Fantasy, Recovery, Consolation and Escape (and that's just for adults)' (*Independent*, 8 September 2001). The article goes on to write about Tolkien's ability to reach the 'inner child' of adults everywhere. We may note here a critique of certain dominant moral evaluations of adulthood; adulthood represents loss as well as gain. There is an attempt to re-negotiate the boundaries between adulthood and childhood and to argue for a greater fluidity and uncertainty. We are, implicitly at least, reminded that it is only in modern times that fairy stories (the very term now signifies an untruth) have become identified with children and childhood. Just as there is an implied critique of the straightforward moral transition from childhood to adulthood so there is also an implied critique of the moral or progressive transition from traditional to modern. Some of these complexities and ambiguities are to be found in writings on the transition to adulthood and in the accounts of some of our respondents.

The uncertainties of adulthood

> It is an open question whether individuals in any given society hold a common notion of adulthood. (Modell et al., 1976: 9)

It is now increasingly common, in writings on the transition to adulthood, to point to the ill-defined nature of adulthood itself. Thus Hutson and Jenkins (1989: 92) find the notion 'curiously ill-defined', something whose meaning is frequently taken for granted. There is a variety of official models of adulthood, reflecting different legal definitions for different purposes such as voting, taking on financial responsibilities, joining the military, buying alcohol and engaging in sexual activity. These complexities are not confined to administrative definitions but are also reflected in expert and popular understandings.

This emphasis on the variety of ways of officially or unofficially defining 'adult' is to be found in other studies (for example, Jones and Wallace, 1992). Morrow and Richards (1996: 10–11) consider four different aspects: political/legal, financial/economic, social/sexual and parenthood, which also closely parallel the dimensions of independence discussed in the previous chapter. Popular understandings are, no doubt, influenced by official definitions just as in complex ways these official definitions reflect some versions of popular beliefs. But there need not be agreement here. The once popular radical slogan 'you're old enough to fight but too young to vote' reflects a perceived lack of fit between definitions.

What is also frequently suggested is that ideas about adulthood have their own history and that constructions of adulthood vary over time as well as between and within societies. To some, the uncertainties about what it means to be an adult are a feature of modern times: 'Adulthood, which once seemed an uneventful, predictable time of life, has more recently come to seem problematic and mysterious' (Swidler, 1980: 120). Swidler links these modern uncertainties with deeper anxieties about the notions of the self and personal identity. Whether the past (itself a highly ambiguous notion) was ever so 'uneventful' or 'predictable' is a matter for some debate.

Philip Ariès' influential, if much debated, history of childhood can also be read as a history of adulthood (Ariès, 1972). Roughly two constructions of adulthood emerge in this work. The first is of a relatively undifferentiated world once the individual had passed infancy. The second, developing between the fourteenth and eighteenth century is a more straightforward distinction between child and adulthood within this post-infancy period. This is not simply a question of chronological age. Wallace and Kovatcheva (1998: 47) write of childhood in pre-industrial northern Europe in these terms: '. . . the determination of youth was not so much *age*, as marriage, gender, inheritance and access to a livelihood.' Again, although they are writing about childhood and youth we can also read this as a statement about adults.

Speaking very roughly (and allowing for differences between northern and southern Europe) we can contrast the complex, if structured, ideas of adulthood in pre-industrial Europe with the growing sense of certainty identified with modern times: 'A few decades ago there were very good reasons for thinking of adulthood as a state of personal identity and completion' (Lee, 2001: 7).

Since then further change, in the direction of greater ambiguity and complexity, has occurred. Lee (and again, it is significant that he is actually writing about childhood) contrasts the standard or 'Fordist' notion of adulthood with the flexibilities of late or post-modern times. It is now difficult to see children and adults as opposites and the distinction between adult 'beings' and child 'becomings' is open to challenge. These debates closely echo the critiques of the dependence/independence distinction discussed in the previous chapter. However, while (in)dependencies are treated as opposites of the same continuum, there is more a sense of adulthood as othering childhood. The adulthood/childhood distinction refers, however indistinctly, to identifiable sections of the population at any point in time. The independence/dependence distinction refers more directly to generalized moral categories. In so far as there is a standard notion of adulthood this can be understood as a Foucauldian 'truth regime'. Adulthood represents a discursive meeting of power and knowledge but one that is increasingly being questioned.

It is relatively easy to identify some of the particular features of late modern society that have contributed to the uncertainties and ambiguities around the notion of adulthood. These have been outlined at several points in this book and include the re-structuring of the labour market, lack of affordable housing and the extension of higher and further education. Other themes include the globalized developments of youth culture and consumption, which implicitly contrast the grey seriousness of adulthood with the cheerful hedonism associated with the transition period. Thus adulthood not only becomes deferred or uncertain; its character as a moral identity may also be called into question. For example, in Brannen and Nilsen (2002), adulthood remains a stage very much located in an indefinite future and their parent's lives are seen as boring and not representing something to be eagerly anticipated. Another way of thinking about this sense of indefiniteness is in terms of an 'extended present' (Oinonen, 2003). The notion of deferring is also mentioned among a few of our respondents. Marc, whose experiences of independence we discussed earlier on, does not regard himself as an adult, and he reckons that being an adult has been pushed back to 35, a change that he equates with the rise of 'lad' culture in England and particularly the magazines such as *FHM* and *Loaded* that promote this:

> going to football, drinking eighteen pints of beer and having a curry. Never in those magazines does it say, you'll be skint because of your mortgage, or – you know? – it's now time to settle down and have kids. It says, right, go out on – get drunk, watch the football, go to clubs and that sort of thing. [Marc L 22 M LH]

However, relatively few of our respondents give a picture of the youthful hedonism sometimes portrayed in popular accounts; even Marc's account above has some ironic detachment from this model.

Notions of adulthood are not uniform and are affected by the usual divisions of social class, gender and ethnicity as well as, perhaps, by other divisions to do with sexuality or ability. Thus, under conditions of modernity, it might be assumed that, for the working class, adulthood was linked to ideas of settling down, having a secure job and moving towards parenthood. Conceptions of adulthood under some sections of the middle class might be associated more with a sense of freedom and openness with 'settling down' being a later stage of adulthood. It is possible that such class divisions, while persisting, have become blurred or more complex under conditions of late modernity. Similarly in the case of gender it can be argued that the older gender divide where adulthood for women was more closely identified with family-based identities such as motherhood in contrast to occupationally based identities for men have also become blurred (Hutson and Jenkins, 1989). Relatively little is known about the impact of ethnic divisions on constructions of adulthood although one may assume that these could continue to be of considerable significance. Again, there is a need for the exploration of the ways in which ideas of adulthood are shaped by different sexualities or different disabilities.

These uncertainties were certainly reflected in some of our interviews in all three settings. In contrast to questions about 'home' or 'independence', we encountered some hesitation and recognition that this was a difficult question to answer:

> Erm, yes and no. [Simon, L 21 M LWP]

> Sometimes, yeah, and sometimes no. [Lisa, L 25 F LH]

Although these two quotations come from Liverpool respondents, similar responses could also be found in the Bilbao or Trondheim transcripts.

In part this reflected a recognition that adulthood was a process rather than a fixed state that our respondents had reached on the basis of their chronological age. A respondent from Bilbao said 'not adult-adult' a recognition that full adulthood lay somewhere in the future. Joar [T 28 M LH] was one of those who felt that the adult stage had not yet been reached: 'But I'm acting adult-like, I think.'

Others argued that it was a question of what you felt. Rachel [L 23 F LWP] had moved back home:

Rachel: I don't think of myself as an adult! [laughs]
Interviewer: You don't?
Rachel: No, not really, I still feel like a little girl.

But she is not sure whether this is because she has moved back home after a period away.

This sense of moving back and forth between adulthood and childhood is common in all three locations. We discuss Lisa's experiences in some detail in Chapter 4. Despite (or maybe because of) the trauma that she has experienced in becoming an 'adult' she still enjoys her ability to forget about being an adult:

And yet me time away from the children, I forget how old I am at times. You know, I've just got, I've got a mad sense of humour and I'm always doing something daft to make my husband laugh, you know, and I always forget how old I am and sometimes, you know its quite funny. I think to meself, flippin' heck, I'm twenty five! [Lisa L 25 F LH]

Espen [T 25 M LH] feels more like a child when he is playing football with his friends. He recognizes that one can be both and that this can be a good thing. Joar [T 28 M LH] similarly refers to 'the small boy inside'. He is also able to live with a sense of uncertainty and probably feels himself to be a 'good-enough' adult:

I actually don't think that I need to become more adult-like you know . . . I think that I have grown up enough . . . I do have my values and norms that guide me, and this I do believe functions quite well . . . And . . . I don't believe that I'm able to fully say what it means to be a fully adult person you know . . . I have found the type of adult figure that best suits me . . . I think (laughs).

We do not know, of course, whether such uncertainties can be attributed to the nature of late modernity. It is possible that people of earlier generations might have said very similar things. But, at least, these responses are consistent with other literature and theorizing. We certainly found some more secure ideas of adulthood but these appear to be linked more strongly to some of the other themes we are discussing.

Adulthood as a moral category

The term 'adult' (and linked terms such as 'mature') are not simply descriptors of a particular stage in life but frequently contain positive moral force. 'Let's be adult about this' is to appeal to certain positive evaluations that consistently rank adult over child or adolescent. Yet the moral evaluation is equivocal. An 'adult movie' or magazine frequently contains more disreputable connotations.

Something of the tensions and ambiguities of the notion of adulthood as a moral category can be found in the transactional analysis of Eric Berne and his once popular *Games People Play* (Berne, 1968). Very simply, Berne identifies three ego states which can be expressed in the simplified terms 'parent', 'adult' and 'child'. Social interactions, therefore, can be between or across these different categories: 'adult/child', 'adult/adult', 'parent/child' and so on. From a sociological perspective the interesting question is how the notion of 'adult' is constructed here.

In the first place it is clear that these are metaphorical usages and ones not directly related to chronological age. Thus Berne is, for the most part, referring to encounters between people who are chronologically 'adult' whatever games they might actually be playing. However he also contrasts 'adult data processing' with the child's spontaneity suggesting that 'children' are rarely adults whereas adults can often be children. Hence there are connections between 'actual' and 'metaphorical' adults although these are not always clear or direct.

Second, we can see two hierarchies involved here. One is the family based hierarchy of parent/child. The other is the wider ordering of adult and child, which are not necessarily based on family identities. While, therefore, 'parent' and 'adult' are separable it is likely that there is always the possibility of some slippage between the two areas of discourse. Thus we may talk of 'father figures', 'mothering' and 'paternalistic' relationships that might be detached from family identities.

Third, although this is more controversial, it would seem that the reader is encouraged to think of 'adult' and 'adult/adult' relationships in broadly positive terms. Thus Berne (1968: 23) refers to 'ego states which are autonomously directed towards object appraisal of reality' and argues that such ego states are 'necessary for survival'. He writes of 'dealing effectively with the outside world' and links adulthood with the idea of autonomy.

It should be stressed that this positive evaluation is not simply attached to the term 'adult' exclusively and that being a 'child' or 'childlike' is not always a matter for disapproval. There can be manipulative adult/adult relationships (the insurance salesperson, for example) and apparent relationships between 'adults' at a sociable level may mask what is in fact the playing out of a 'parent/child' game. There is plenty of room for moral complexity and ambiguity in the games people play.

Nevertheless, it is difficult not to detect an overall positive endorsement of 'adult' and adult relationships and, although Berne claims that transactional analysis is free from any particular cultural context, the term does seem to have affinities with Weberian models of rationality. If it be the case that the term 'adult' is positively evaluated then this may be the outcome of the development of rational modernity. Going beyond the more careful analysis of Berne to more popular representations it might be seen that the positive adult construction is not only bourgeois but also white and male and probably able bodied and heterosexual as well. Further, the adult should not be 'too old'.

The persistence of a positive moral evaluation of the category 'adult' may in part be behind some of the more recent concerns about prolonged adolescence or delayed adulthood. For a variety of structural and cultural reasons (some of which are explored elsewhere), young people are sometimes seen to be unwilling or unable to assume the status of adulthood and all the rights and duties which are associated with this term: political, financial, parental, sexual and so on. As we shall see in the next section, adulthood is liked to a variety of other positive values and an apparent rejection of the former may also been seen as a flight from responsibility, independence and commitment.

How do our respondents view adulthood as a moral category? We have already seen that there is considerable uncertainty about the term and its relevance to our interviewees' life-course stage. Some, as we have seen, clearly adopt a Berne-like understanding of a 'child' and an 'adult' co-existing within the same individual. What positive endorsement we have for the idea of adulthood comes through its constructed links with values to do with independence, autonomy and responsibility rather than any clearly stated 'reality principle'. A mother of one of our Norwegian respondents, for example, stated that she 'would either use the words mature or immature'. Another Norwegian mother feels that her daughter is 'much more sensible'. Positive evaluations of adulthood do not necessarily depend on age. Marte is 18 and living at home and longs to be an adult and manage on her own. However, she does not see it in wholly positive terms and that: 'you have to clean up after yourself and pay your bills also.'

We did come across a few highly articulate rejections of adulthood. Lapsus (Bilbao) was aged 27 at the time of interview and living with friends. He was a student with a grant and worked as a drama teacher and in a bar. He was therefore an example of someone who, in the Spanish context, had made an unorthodox exit from the parental home. He does not see himself as an adult and feels that 'to be an adult you have to be serious, grey, have a sombrero, work 8 hours and have a routine life and live a conventional life'. He associates leaving home with the achievement of independence but not with becoming an adult.

Ben Obi (Trondheim) is aged 26 and lives at his parents' house. He is planning to move soon and sees his present stay at home as a transitional arrangement, which is economic and practical. He is training to be a pilot. He laughs when asked whether he sees himself as an adult: 'no, then you have this A4 life so to speak and boring . . . and settling down you know . . . I'm still youthful . . .' He sees his parents as adults and feels that he is not like them. Living at home might, he agrees, be something to do with his lack of adult identification.

Such identifications of adulthood with routine and boredom were rare in our accounts. At the same time, it was difficult to find any strong positive endorsements of being an adult or longings to achieve this state. Its status as a moral category, on its own, does seem uncertain. But perhaps this moral evaluation derives from its association with other prized values.

Links with other moral categories

These other prized values include categories that are strongly linked to ideas of adulthood such as 'maturity' but also a range of other ideas including the various dimensions of independence, discussed in the previous chapter, and ideas of responsibility. Indeed, it could be argued that these other terms are generally preferred to the term 'adult' because of uncertainties about the definitions and evaluations of this latter status. Certainly, it would seem, the idea of adulthood gains through being linked to these other values although the connections between them are not always straightforward. Thus there can be a straight preference for, say, 'independence' as against adulthood or it may be argued that the achievement of a measure of independence does not always imply adulthood and vice versa.

In the first place it can be readily argued that there are differences between adulthood and maturity (Irwin, 1995: 60). Generally speaking, adulthood refers more to formal definitions and understandings that are linked, however loosely, to chronological age. Maturity, on the other hand, is more clearly a kind of moral evaluation or something that refers to capacities rather than status. Thus, for Freud, maturity represented the capacity to love and to work – that is to enter into intimate relationships involving caring and inter-dependence and to engage, actively and coherently, in the wider social world (Smelser, 1980). To be adult (at least in terms of some definitions) is not necessarily to be mature and it is possible for an individual to act in a mature way despite lacking any of the formal qualifications for adulthood.

Second, it can be seen that while 'adult' and 'adulthood' may be points of departure people are rarely content to remain there. When asked about what it means to be an adult, several of Hutson and Jenkins' young respondents referred to terms such as 'responsibility' and 'independence' (Hutson and Jenkins, 1989: 95–103). Similar moves can be found in the accounts of other researchers. Thus La Fontaine, in common with many others, stresses that adulthood is 'always a matter of social definition rather than physical maturity' and goes on to argue that adult status 'confers rights and responsibilities on the individual' (La Fontaine, 1986: 19). Ribbens-McCarthy et al. (2003: 53–4) stress that 'adult' and 'child' are moral categories and, on the basis of their qualitative study of step-parenthood, point to some of the dimensions of the moral status of 'adult'. These include being morally accountable, putting the needs of children first (thus strongly linked to parenthood), and being in a position to make moral choices (Westberg, 2004). In a complex theoretical argument, Irwin links notions of adulthood and youth to the processes of social reproduction. These terms refer to the ways in which individuals resource their day-to-day livelihoods and the reproduction of households and new generations. They refer to 'the ways in which dependence and independence are resourced' (Irwin, 1995: 7). Irwin takes a more straightforwardly materialist perspective on these categories. The important point here is that she stresses that dependence and independence need some material base and resourcing and that we understand the terms youth and adulthood to be various mixes of dependence and independence.

In all kinds of ways, therefore, both theoretically and in terms of more everyday perceptions, there are strong links between ideas of adulthood and independence. However, our interview data suggest some complexities in the relationship between adulthood and independence. Bergante, one of our Spanish informants, is aged 31 and living at home. He has a good job but no partner and recognizes the latter as being one of the main reasons for not leaving home. He feels that adulthood and independence are not the same thing and that adulthood is the more difficult term. He recognizes, for example, that a couple may lose independence once they start living together but that they are still two adults. Looking at his own situation he recognizes a certain lack of independence through living in the parental home but does not see that this has implications for his adult status. Though he jokes about maybe having a 'Peter Pan' syndrome he is somewhat defensive about both his self-recognition of and others treating him like an 'adult'. This sense of adulthood is not simply based upon chronological age but reflects a fact of being able to make one's own decisions. However it is interesting that his definition of 'adulthood' as '*una persona capaz de tomar sus propias decisiones*' (a person capable of taking their own decisions) is similar to how other Spanish respondents define independence, reflecting the overlap between the two. The linkages between adulthood and independence will therefore depend on how these two are defined, and in some cases both identities are used to refer to much the same qualities, though in different ways. Much of the uncertainty (and not simply in Bilbao) reflects ambiguities and complexities within the ideas of independence and adulthood.

In all three locations there is a strong identification of adulthood and responsibility. This itself is a complex term that includes taking responsibility for oneself (and hence is linked to independence) and taking responsibility for others. Emerging out of these is a sense of being a responsible person. To take responsibility for oneself is to take on a whole host of decisions, small and large, which had hitherto been largely handled by one's parents. It is having no one else to blame apart for oneself if things go wrong and it is claiming ownership of one's actions. Catherine [L 26 F LH] says: 'I'm getting up in the mornings now instead of staying in bed all day, and I'm taking responsibility for myself rather than trying to fall back on my Mum all the time.'

Jane [L 20 F LH] also notes some of the everyday things: 'just the fact that being on your own and having to cope, having to do it, get yourself up every day, cook your dinner, you know. And make the house look clean. Erm, things like that, say.'

She feels a sense of pride in being able to cope better than her parents thought she could. As we discussed in the previous chapter, this recognition of 'coping' is closely related to her sense of independence.

One key aspect of taking responsibility for oneself is to do with the management of money. In discussing financial independence we argued that managing money (however little) was at least as important as having 'enough' money to live an independent life. This theme also emerges when we consider adulthood. It is a question of budgeting, paying bills and generally coming to grips with a world of organizations and bureaucracies that have their own timetables and expectations. In some cases these are skills that are learnt at college in halls of residence or shared housing. Catherine, for example, notes that:

> And the first year in halls we erm, we'd all put a fiver in and go shopping at Netto and feed ourselves for a week on fiver, so we were like really organized and I think it was a team, like the team work, which felt like a team-building exercise.

The negotiation of adulthood

As we have argued, the word 'negotiation' has increasingly been used in the context of family studies. In some cases, the negotiation might be relatively overt with various claims and counter-claims being made on both sides. If we consider everyday concerns such as a young person's time keeping and how long she should stay out at night (see also Chapter 3) we might see all kinds of conditions and justifications moving back and forth between parent and child. We can see such negotiations as being about the overt question to hand – when she should be expected to return from a night out with her friends – but also about the status of the parties involved. This includes the young person's status as a near-adult and the moral rights and duties attached to being an adult and a parent. It is, of course, true that, as Hockey and James (2003) argue, the very terms 'adult' and 'child' are products of relations of power within the family and the wider political or moral order. However, these statuses are not fixed (children grow older) and some degree of negotiation is always possible.

Negotiations may be much less overt of course, as much a matter of tone of voice, gesture, facial expressions and so on as of more explicit claims on both sides. But even where the negotiation might be overt (whether the young person in the parental home should pay something for her keep and, if so, how much) other less open notions of adulthood and responsibility are also being negotiated.

If negotiations are taking place, who are the parties in this process? Obviously, as has already been suggested, we are concerned with the young people at home or leaving home and their parents. But there is also negotiation taking place between the young person concerned and many other significant, or less significant, others. These may include siblings, other family members, friends, people and work or simply people in the street. There will almost certainly be some kind of internal debate or negotiation taking place within the young person herself.

In qualitative research in particular, the negotiation also takes place between the respondent (either a young person or a parent) and the interviewer. For example:

Interviewer: You also made a comment there about growing up. Um . . .
Ally: I need to do that.
Interviewer: So do you consider yourself to be an adult?
Ally: Um, sort of . . .

Ally, who is 21 and living at home, then goes on to elaborate what she means by 'sort of', in that although her age and the fact that she plans to get married soon make her feel like an 'adult', the fact that her parents 'mollycoddle' her and she relies on their opinions negates her sense of being an 'adult'.

Another example comes from an interview with a Norwegian mother whose daughter has left home:

Interviewer: Another word is 'adult' . . . do you look upon [name] as a grown up person?
Anna: Yes I do . . .
Interviewer: When did you start 'doing' that?

Anna: That has gone gradually . . .
Interviewer: Did this last until you 'left' each other?
Anna: No. She became an adult while she was staying at home, I think
so . . .

In these examples, which can be multiplied, we see two issues working
together. In the first place there is whether the individual being interviewed
or under discussion can be defined as an adult. In the second place, there is the
very nature of the identity 'adult' itself. These meanings are produced, tested
and modified, in the exchanges, or negotiations, between the interviewer and
the subject.

The most important negotiations take place with significant others among
whom parents are the most important. There are numerous accounts of young
people who feel that their relationship with their parents (or at least one parent) has changed over time and that they are now more likely to be regarded as
an adult. The signs of these changes are various and often quite subtle. One
Norwegian respondent, for example, talked about shifting from drinking soda
at Christmas to drinking red wine. Several others talked about a sense of
having 'adult' conversations, a shift, in the terms of transactional analysis
from adult-child to adult-adult. Some individuals feel that these changes took
place after the young person had left home and the parents could see that she
or he was capable of making a go of it on their own. But leaving home was not
always necessary for this transition to take place. María [B 27 F LH] left home
to live with a partner, itself an unusual act in the Spanish context. She recalls
conflict and tension between herself and her parents but felt that it was
important to sort out her relationships with her parents before she left home:

> at that moment just before leaving home, the advantages were that
> . . . we got on very well, we talked quite a lot . . . we began to have a
> reconciliation; they talked more about their life, I also of mine, and
> . . . up until then the relation had been a little like father-baby daugh-
> ter, so to speak, they didn't tell you anything, they didn't say anything
> to you, and then it began to be more an adult relationship.

This process continued after she left home as she began to make her own
decisions and her parents saw that she was doing this.

Katrine [T 25 F LWP] is another example of someone living at home who
feels that she is regarded as an adult:

> maybe this has something to do with the fact that my father is a
> lawyer and knows a person's rights when he or she turns eighteen . . .
> But I think they trusted me a lot, them feeling this going well
> enough. They felt that I had grown up enough then, and it also

looked for them that I was able to take care of myself and I had never been involved in anything stupid either. Them trusting the kind of person who I had turned into then, managing on my own you know . . .

Indeed, in these two examples it would seem that, during the period of living in the parental home, the parents were able to pick up evidence of adulthood on a day-to-day basis and to alter their behaviour accordingly.

On the other hand, leaving the parental home does not necessarily mean that one will automatically be treated as an adult by one's parents. Hannah (Liverpool, 29) left home to marry after several moves in and out of the parental home. She feels that planning to get married was a crucial step although she points to differences between her mother and her father. Her father still sees her as a little girl but 'my mum knows I'm a woman and independent now'.

That relationships with parents are frequently crucial in the development of a sense of adulthood and that this process does not always go smoothly should not cause much surprise. Everything from popular advice columns to psychological or psycho-analytical texts would say the same thing. What is important here is the idea of negotiation, which stresses the active role of the young person in developing a sense of adulthood within the context of the parental home.

Negotiations with parents take place within a context of a relationship that is, in varying degrees, structured by power. A sense of equality – adult to adult – may be the outcome of the negotiation process but is not the point of departure. This differs from negotiations with others where the power relationship may be muted or apparently absent. Relationships with siblings may be structured by age and hence carry with them some elements of the parent-child relationship. Thus the experience of caring for a younger sibling might contribute to a sense of adulthood within the family context. Or, the younger or older sibling might provide some point of comparison against which to measure the distance one has travelled in the direction of adulthood.

Friends may also provide reference groups, points of comparison. The experience of friends having left home may heighten a sense of being left behind in a state of non-adulthood. Alternatively, friends (fellow students, for example) may seem to be stuck in some adolescent world in comparison with oneself. Sarah [L 21 F LH], for example, left home to go to university having already had some work experience in Europe. Prior to her going to university 'the circles I moved, everyone was a bit older. And coming here, everyone is sort of just eighteen. Er, I found myself really irritated about how, the inability to look after themselves.'

Beyond the significant others in the parental home and the circle of friends, there are numerous, often nameless, individuals who confirm or undermine a sense of adulthood. Rachel [L 23 F LWP] is living at home and does not see herself as an adult. But contacts with the outside world can be confusing:

> But also I think even last year, I just still felt like a little girl. You know, you hear 'mind out for the lady' and you think, where's the lady, or something, and oh, they're talking about me! [laughs] But I am, I know I'm an adult, but I don't feel like one, really . . . But then, in school, I did get asked by the dinner lady if I was a pupil. I said 'no, I'm teaching here'! [laughs]

Similarly, encounters at work (supposedly an adult activity) can undermine a sense of adulthood if the fellow workers are all older or more experienced. Lynn [L 35 F LWP] as we discussed in Chapter 3 is the oldest respondent living at home. sometimes she feels like an adult (when she is with her friends' children, for example) but mostly she still sees herself as 'sort of twenties'. However, she is still the youngest person in the office and single and feels 'they talk down to me like I'm a bit of a kid'.

The notion of adulthood, and the extent to which it applies in any particular situation, is negotiated on a day-to-day basis with numerous others, significant and less significant. As has been illustrated, these 'others' are not always providing a unified or coherent picture. In addition to these identifiable 'others' – family, friends, people at work – we can also refer to what Mead has called the 'generalized other', a theme that we discuss at greater length in the next chapter. As the term suggests, this 'other' is in part generalized through these numerous other encounters and relationships, although there is something over and above the sum of all these negotiations. An illustration of this is provided by an interview with Vito, a Spanish man of 28 living at home with his parents:

> Vito: For my age I don't consider myself to be very adult, but . . .
> Interviewer: Let's see, could you explain to me what you mean when you say 'for my age'?
> Vito: Well, there are people who are my age who live alone, including some who are married, have kids, then . . . good . . . I don't know if you would call them more adult, I don't know . . .

It is not entirely clear whether Vito is referring to actual individuals who could be identified if asked. But clearly some degree of generalization is taking place. In this case, the 'generalized other' does not provide a clear picture but, rather, underlines a common sense of uncertainty when it comes to defining adulthood and its more immediate relevance.

It is here that the negotiation is necessarily at its most metaphorical.

Nevertheless, it can be seen as part of the wider negotiation process, a testing of self and identity against the constructed sense of what others are doing and believing. Ultimately, of course, the negotiation becomes an internalized process, a debate within an individual. This sense of an internal debate can sometimes be indicated through qualitative interviews.

Another way of looking at the process of becoming an adult is in terms of a sense of living in an adult world. In the words of one of the Liverpool respondents: 'I think you erm, can't become fully adult until you move out of the house and see things for yourself. And the way the world is. And my financial situation and things like that' [Amber L 22 F LH]. This is partly a sense of living in a world that is largely peopled by adults, but adults who are not immediately responsible for your wellbeing. It is partly also a question of doing 'adult things'. These adult things are numerous and varied; examples may be caring for others, doing some voluntary work in the community, paying bills and taking out a mortgage. One particular example may involve a slight reversal of roles when parents come to visit their son or daughter who has left home and has separate accommodation. Another way of considering these numerous experiences is in the use of the complex word 'experience':

I mean my experiences have been really bad and they have been tough on me and I've been through a lot . . . but, they have helped me, they've made me grow up a lot and realize that life isn't as sweet as what everyone might think it is. [Helen L 17 F LH]

Constructions of the adult world, and of one's place in this world, also involve constructions of the non-adult world. Roja, a young Spanish woman who left home at 23, makes a contrast which to some extent revolves around an adult/non-adult distinction: 'Then . . . I see that when I speak, as well, with my friends there are issues or things in life that still they haven't begun to understand and that I have already lived and I understand.'

The possibility of making these kinds of contrasts in part reflects the fact that there is not a smooth, integrated or coherent transition to adulthood in modern society. People of the same age may have had different experiences and leaving the parental home is not always straightforwardly identified with the attainment of full adult status. Jane, from Liverpool, states this in gendered terms: 'like if my brother was older than me, I couldn't honestly see, I couldn't see him doing anything. He just wouldn't have a clue. But I think there's a difference between boys and girls.'

This contrast, which is elaborated later in the same part of the interview, is partly in terms of activities (going off with mates or football as against 'housebuilding and things') and partly in terms of attitude. Some of our other interviewees also made the same kind of gendered contrast. But even without the gender theme there are comparisons made between an individual's present situation and the lives and expectations of peers and others who apparently live in the same adult world.

It is important to distinguish between those whose behaviour and attitudes still signify membership of a pre-adult world and those who can knowingly slip into this pre-adult world from time to time. As followers of transactional analysis might argue it is sometimes both possible and desirable for an adult to act in a 'child-like' (rather than 'childish') manner. This is a more 'carnivalesque' form of acting that re-affirms the nature and value of adulthood while temporarily dropping the adult mask. It is as if the assumption of adult responsibilities – family, financial obligations, employment – can be rewarded with periods of child-like release. The adult is able to move between states; being an adult may mean not being an adult.

A case study: Hilde

Hilde, from Trondheim, was 27 years old at the time of her interview. She was working full-time as a teacher, having completed her university education. She had left home twice but was living in the parental home partly because of a fatal accident involving her sister. Hilde felt that she should return home and support her parents but now feels that it is time to be moving out again. As with some of the other Norwegian respondents, she had several rooms of her own within the parental home although she shared the kitchen and the bathroom.

Hilde feels that she is independent despite living in the parental home and she contrasts her present situation with earlier periods at home. The fact that she has had some periods away from home, she feels, has contributed to her sense of independence. This is despite the fact that she acknowledges that her contributions to living expenses are less than she would pay elsewhere. There was an agreement with her mother that Hilde should save from her earnings in order to facilitate her move later on. Had she not saved this money, her mother would have charged her rent. For Hilde, then, being independent was more a sense of personal autonomy rather than complete financial independence.

An interesting symbol of her relationship with her parents was to do with the car. She says that one of the positive things about living at home is that if there is anything wrong with the car ('changing the oil and so on') she can ask her father to look at it. The car was originally her mother's but she did not have a great need for it so Hilde took the car over, paying the tax and insurance. As Hilde works outside the city and travels over 60 miles each day, this is important for her sense of independence even if she does not yet take complete responsibility for the vehicle.

When it comes to a sense of adulthood, Hilde has considerable uncertainties and her interview shows the important role that 'others' play in constructing or deconstructing a sense of being an adult. In relation to her parents she feels that she is regarded as an adult: 'My parents most probably look upon me as another grown up adult . . . I'm still their kid, but I'm also an adult . . . They know that I have managed on my own, having a job and so on.' The fact that she spend some time away from home has probably helped here, she argues.

Yet she states that she does not feel herself to be an adult and her elaboration of this feeling clearly states the complex ways in which others, in this case at the work place, contribute to this sense of uncertainty:

> I have never looked upon myself as that much of an adult actually, so I got this feeling then, or you know, something like 'nowadays I have to' . . . Or as a teacher I have to be an adult person . . . You are supposed to be a sort of role model then, and I have to start to reflect a little upon this, and the things being a little . . . like this autumn when I worked as an assistant beside where I lived. At some school nearby, I didn't feel that comfortable to go shopping after for example some beer if some of my pupils were to see it you know. It's not like I'm having some need to tell them that I'm not drinking, but anyway . . . actually I don't know . . . I did feel a little bit . . . I think its OK that the pupils are where the school is, and I'm at this place you know. And also the part with meeting the parents at school. I'm closer to their children when you think of age than I'm to them actually . . . There are parents there who are as old as my parents, and there I'm to tell them how their children behave and so on.

This is a good illustration of some of the complexities involved. Not only does Hilde feel more of an adult in some situations rather than others but she is also conducting a kind of debate within herself and with the interviewer. It is also possible to see part of the process of constructing a generalized other here, in that the parents and children are aggregated rather than given particular or individualized identities.

At the same time, Hilde does have some sense of adulthood as a moral identity. This is partially indicated in this quotation but becomes more explicit later when she talks about being an adult role-model: 'I would like to be an adult, someone who is respecting them [children at school] and someone who also takes their opinions a little seriously if they say their thoughts.' But this is some stage in the future. Hilde is sure that she is an independent being, despite still living in the parental home, although she continues to have doubts about her adult status.

Concluding remarks

Much of the current literature as well as the interview material cited here points to considerable complexity around the notion of 'adulthood'. On the whole there seems to be a recognition that adulthood is a moral identity, linked to other values to do with maturity and taking responsibility for oneself and for others. One or two respondents have reservations about this identity and many have doubts about its applicability in terms of their present status. For several, adulthood seems to be some stage in the future, as yet ill-defined. Adulthood is not clearly associated with chronological age, nor is it necessarily associated with leaving the parental home or with independence.

There is a sense in which adulthood can be identified with taking a place in the everyday world or, even, the 'real' world. (This might reflect the relative marginalization of children and children's experiences in modern societies.) The notion of everyday life is a complex one (Morgan, 2004) but two aspects might seem to be relevant. One is being in touch with what are regarded as key events or experiences in the human life-course. These include sexuality, birth and parenthood, bereavement, caring for others and so on. Sexuality is almost absent from our accounts but there seems to be a clear sense that caring for others (partners, children) is an important element in adult identity. The other dimension of everyday life is a sense of the routine, the mundane and the relatively predictable. (Clearly, such an account is limited in terms of historical time and geographical space.) Adulthood is linked to this sense of the everyday through talk of paying bills, keeping an orderly house, adhering to relatively predictable timetables and so on. It is possibly this sense of adulthood that is subject to some resistance. To be adult is to be in what is defined as an adult world, doing adult things and having adult experiences. The fact that these worlds and practices do not always completely overlap contributes to the uncertainties about defining adulthood in late modern society.

7 Connected transitions: significant and generalized others

One of the signs of passing youth is the birth of a sense of fellowship with other human beings as we take our place among them.

Virginia Woolf, *The Times Literary Supplement*, 30 November 1916

Throughout this book we have stressed the importance of *not* treating young people's lived experiences in isolation from significant others. Young people make sense of the three main themes of this book – home, independence and adulthood – through their relationship with others. For example, many young people identified home spaces through family or other intimate relations. While independence might, by definition, initially exclude others, in practice the concept of inter-dependencies is often more meaningful than independence itself. Finally, young people's sense of adulthood is legitimated through recognition by significant others. In this chapter we seek to draw together the significance of social relations on young people's lives. We consider how leaving home is rarely a solo project, but is one that might involve a whole host of other people, as well as processes and structures that are involved or implicated in young people's lives. These include family, of course, but also friends and peer groups, family friends, teachers, youth workers and other adults in authority positions. Many encounters will be formalized and determined by prevailing policies and structures and our discussion of social relations will also draw on these.

We start this chapter by emphasizing our basic premise, that young people do not leave home on their own but a whole host of different actors are brought into play. Partly reflecting the design of our research, we are able to provide a very rich account of the importance of family members, particular parents, on young people's experiences of both living at home and leaving home. Yet our interest in exploring the embeddedness of leaving-home practices is not simply to measure the extent to which parents assist children in the process of leaving, or supporting them at home, nor to document the different kinds of support that young people might receive. In line with the overall agenda of this book, it is to explore how practices of support and young people's social relations are contextualized.

In seeking to theorize these accounts of support and networks, we start from the perspective of writings on social capital, particularly Bourdieu's approach, which seems most relevant for our purposes (Morrow, 1999). We can take Bourdieu's treatment of capital to distinguish between the different kinds of support that young people may or may not receive: that is young people may acquire 'capital' within the family that is economic, social, cultural or symbolic (Bourdieu, 1997), and that differential acquisition of capital is related to the perpetuation of inequalities between families (Bourdieu and Passeron, 1977). Yet distinguishing between different types and amounts of 'capital' still leaves the question of accounting for how support is negotiated and the significance of social relations on all family members. As Morrow (1999) comments on the social capital literature, young people and children are treated as outcomes, not active agents in the production of capital. For example we do not want to restrict ourselves to a linear flow of capital from parents to children.

Moreover, we recognize that the process of negotiation and maintenance of social relations is not simply determined by the availability of resources, but that there are moral negotiations that go on within families that might lead to parents not providing support (being 'cruel to be kind') or children rejecting what is offered, so to demonstrate autonomy. However, staying with Bourdieu, capital is only half of his theory of practice and is intricately linked to the related concept of habitus. In moving towards a more dynamic approach to family support, it is, as Morrow (1999: 757) also argues, important to relate capital to practices: 'we can move forward, I suggest, by coupling Bourdieu's original formulation of social capital as in relation with other forms of capital as rooted in the practices of everyday life, with a view of children having agency (albeit constrained); thus linking micro-social and macro-social structural factors.'

Bourdieu describes habitus as a 'product of history', it puts the past in the present through ensuring the 'active presence of past experiences, which, deposited in each organism in the form of schemes of perception, thought and action tend to guarantee the "correctness" of practices and their constancy over time' (Bourdieu, 1990 : 54). Habitus is therefore a dynamic and reflexive concept that recognizes how practices can be strategic in that they may be conditioned to achieve pre-determined outcomes and replicate accepted forms of behaviour (Crossley, 2001). 'How' to operationalize capital, and in our case to transfer resources between family members, or other social networks, may be treated as part of habitus, and as such is a set of practices that is rooted in both the past and the present. As we have discussed elsewhere, 'correct' practices may be constructed within families as well as communities; family members do not simply make use of the 'tool kits' provided by the wider culture but also adapt and elaborate their own cultural resources (Holdsworth, 2004). Institutional practices are relevant here, particularly the ways in which support for young people is incorporated into social assistance programmes. Our point here is that we need to consider both the actual payments that young people do or might potentially receive and how assumptions about the appropriateness of assistance within welfare schemes, reflects wider believes about how to provide (or not provide) support.

Our final fine-tuning of Bourdieu reflects the criticism that habitus relies too much on the unconscious, that correct forms of practices are internalized and unquestionably and, potentially unknowingly, reproduced (Crossley, 2001; Reay, 2004). Yet in our analysis of how young people negotiate transitions, conversations with others are important – not just with families and friends but also conversations with oneself, where young people think not just about what 'other' people are doing, but how other people think about them. We find, in our discussions with young people, accounts of a very active internalization of 'correct forms of practice' and use the concept of the generalized other to explore this dimension of embeddedness.

Family

Recognizing the significance of the family in the lives of young people has emerged as a key theme in transition studies in recent years (see, for example, Gillies, 2000), and the importance of the family on young people's outcomes is also a common theme among our respondents. Oddvar is a widowed father from Trondheim, who remarks how family (and particularly parents) can make all the difference, yet this difference is not necessarily just about resources:

> it is important to have a home, and it is important to have a close family . . . People who end up on the streets . . . it often happens to those who, where either parents had split up, or them not knowing at all where their parents were, and some also had parents who never questioned where they went and so on you know . . . And then they felt they had no one to answer to. [Oddvar T P M LH]

There are differing approaches to incorporating how families can make a difference on young people's experiences. In the transition model, family context often determines the starting point of the transition phase and the resources that young people have access to during processes of change. Yet there is considerable variation in how family resources are conceptualized. They may be reduced to economic criteria (for example, see Goldscheider and Goldscheider, 1999, Chapter 8) or, following Bourdieu, include other forms of capital such as cultural, social and symbolic capital (De Jong Gierveld et al.,

1991). As outlined above, our use of Bourdieu is not just restricted to identifying different forms of capital and how they are exchanged, but how these exchanges (or even withdrawal of support) are part of the 'correct' practices of habitus. In doing so, and following several other researchers, we aim to avoid the problem inherent to many approaches to socialization whereby family is taken as a rather static entity, particularly when conceptualizing young people's relationships within families (Jenks, 1982; Alanen, 1988; Brannen and O'Brien, 1996; James and Prout, 1997). Family sometimes emerges as a black box out of which social inequalities are perpetuated, and there is not much sense of an ongoing dialogue between family members. Moreover, the concept of family is one that is located in young people's past, rather than in their present and future. Yet, as we have argued throughout this book, family cannot be reduced to a system of resources out of which young people 'emerge'. Family is not a system of resources (or lack of resources), and if family is taken as a structure at all, it is very much an active one. For this reason, we find it useful to talk about 'family practices' (Morgan, 1996), that is the various ways in which – and contexts within which – people 'do' family. This approach to family life has emerged as a dominant theme in family studies in recent years. The emphasis has shifted towards how family *cannot* be taken for granted (Bernardes, 1998); relations and inter-familial support are viewed as negotiated and situational (Finch and Mason, 1993). As such how family members interact and, crucially, the kinds and types of support that members provide, are not determined by fixed rules but are negotiated between members and are highly contextual. Family support is conditional and depends on circumstances; it may be subject to restrictions. This approach to family demands a more responsive approach to family relations in that we cannot assume that 'the family' is something that is fixed in time or space and that it is just young people who are moving on; that all family members, however defined, are also part of the process. It is also just as important to consider how parents respond to change, or the possibility of change, and how this impacts on them.

As we explore in this chapter, the ways in which parents give support and young people receive it is often strategic in that it seeks to reinforce a certain set of practices and behaviour, or habitus, over and above the more immediate concerns of giving children money to help pay the rent or buy a sofa. We see the strategic form of this behaviour in how children are expected to act in response to receiving support. Our argument is that it is not simply how help is provided, through flows of economic and social capital, that distinguishes between different contexts. It is also as much a question of the differences between the expectations about what young people can or should learn through these processes and how these experiences are constructed.

As outlined in Chapter 2, one of the main reasons for choosing Britain, Spain and Norway as the three countries in our study was because of the different family 'cultures' or systems that are recognized as characteristic of those countries. Much has been written about the difference between the northern and southern family in terms of what it means to young people (Cavalli and Galland, 1995; Jurado Guerrero and Naldini, 1997; Reher, 1998) and the image of young southern males (less commonly females) still living with parents in their late 20s and early 30s is quite common in the British media. Yet while stereotypes of family life in northern and southern Europe emphasize the differential amount of support that is available to the younger generation, in practice we find an almost universal recognition of the importance of the family and parents in particular. We suggest that it is not so much a question of what family members do for each other that differ (and here we need to consider what children do for parents as well as *vice versa*) but the conditions under which help and support are given that vary between different contexts.

Parental support: capital in context

In Spain, given common preconceptions about southern family life, we are not surprised to find that parents and young people alike are strong advocates of family solidarity and often accept the importance of support uncritically. The archetypal Spanish model is one where children are supported in and outside of the home. As Rosa, a Spanish mother, describes, when her daughter lived at home she did not expect her, or her sister, to contribute to household chores.

> . . . the truth is that [daughter's name], didn't help. Very little. Because it is either that she couldn't; because in the morning if she was going to university she can't; if she is giving classes, well she can't. Well, what I want to say is that she . . . if she is working on something she can't do the housework as well. It isn't important to me that they don't help. I want them to lead their lives because . . . we have a small house! [Rosa B P F LH]

After leaving home, Rosa continues to support her daughter, and often picks things up for her when out shopping:

> No, no, no, no. She does not ask. I have gone out and I have called her on the mobile in the supermarket to tell her '– [daughter's name], we are in the supermarket, do you need anything? what do you need', – then, 'now I don't think I need anything Mum, but maybe I need such and such a thing'. And it is like this.

As both these extracts illustrate, Rosa is a little hesitant in admitting how she supports her daughter. When describing how she does not expect her daughter to contribute to housework, she makes excuses: 'the house is small', 'they have busy lives and don't have time to do housework'. When describing her shopping practices she describes how her daughter will initially respond by rejecting her parents' offer of help. Whether Rosa is concerned to make an impression for the interviewer, or if she is convincing herself that her actions are appropriate, in providing 'excuses' for her daughter's behaviour, is not clear. While Rosa's case very much represents the expected relationship between parents and children in Spain, we do at least gain some sense of how these relationships are open to some negotiation, or at least justification. However, the process of negotiation is quite different to that which we might encounter in other contexts in that Rosa does not challenge her daughter's behaviour. She accepts the excuses that she herself provides. For her part, Rosa's daughter acknowledges the support that she receives from her parents and at times how she benefits from this. She is, though, also aware of feeling trapped by her family, that she delayed leaving home precisely because her parents were prepared to make excuses as to why she did not have to leave. As such the overall practice of negotiation in Rosa's family is one that is quite rigid, with little room for manoeuvre on either side.

Often it is the experiences that stand out as being different that are most informative as to how culturally dominant patterns are reproduced. While most of the Spanish families that we spoke to described similar family practices to Rosa's family, Felipe and Marta, a lower-middle-class couple from Bilbao, explained how they attempted to make their daughter pay her way at home:

Marta: We told her an amount [to pay] and she began to give us almost half of this until we said to her 'this cannot be'.
Felipe: It is important to say that when we established the amount with her it was not done in an arbitrary way. I can explain.
Marta: We did a budget and divided it up.
Felipe: With numbers, with numbers, and we made a note of the budget for this house. [Felipe and Marta B Ps LH].

Felipe and Marta divided their family budget by the number of adults in employment and expected all their children who were in employment to make the same contribution. However, their strategy backfired as, according to their account of their daughters' departure, she chose to leave home rather than pay board in the manner stipulated by her parents. Parents do not, therefore, have free reign to dictate their own terms; if these go against what is commonly done elsewhere they will not necessarily be accepted by other family members and will be harder to enforce. Felipe and Marta recognize that their attitude is not common among their friends and neighbours. Felipe's views are quite clear: that in not asking children to help they are learning 'bad ways' and are happy to let others run around for them. Yet he recognizes that among his contemporaries the most common reason for not asking for any money from adult children is that parents do not need any extra money. Many parents who we spoke to in all three locations rationalized their acceptance that they should not expect adult children to contribute to the household economy with concern over how the much 'harder' it is for young people to establish an independent residence, both in terms of the cost of leaving home, and also the precarious nature of the youth labour market.

Turning to Norway, the stereotype of the distant and emotionless Scandinavian family is as widespread and as resonant as the over-protective Spanish family. Yet this stereotypical view was not something that Norwegians themselves would recognize. For example, Joar's [T 28 M LH] family lives on a remote island in northern Norway (with only 17 inhabitants). His father works in the fishing industry and his mother in a bakery. His parents moved to the island when he was 14. Prior to that he had lived in Oslo and Trondheim. Yet he did not live on the island for long, due to limited educational opportunities there, and he left home at 16 to pursue his studies. According to his description, leaving home at such a young age was helped considerably by having supportive parents:

> Well, out in the islands where we lived, it was normal for 16 year olds to leave home actually . . . and I don't think I was sort of mature enough to leave at that age either . . . So you are very dependent on having stable parents I think, who are there for you, helping you and taking care of you then . . .

His parents therefore helped him from a distance, and leaving home at such a young age was greatly facilitated through the support he received from his parents. Joar's experience may be contrasted with that of Carlota [B 28 F LH] who left her parental home in Galicia in northwest Spain when she was 12 to live with her sister in order to go to school in Bilbao. Carlota's parents are farmers and worked abroad when she was little (at that time she lived with her grandparents). Like Joar, she left home at a young age because of limited educational opportunities in the locality of her parental home. However, unlike Joar, rather than being supported by her parents from a distance, her older sister and brother-in-law were *in loco parentis* and took responsibility not just for her board and lodging but her personal development and conduct. For example, she describes how her sister and brother-in-law asserted their authority in a similar way to that which her parents would have done, if she had lived with them, such as agreeing times for getting home at night. Carlota 'left' her sister's home when she was 28 when she married her husband Jon. While she left her parental home at a very young age, she was not expected to conform to a different life-course pattern on account of this. Rather, she acquired an 'alternative' family, which she did not 'leave' until she was much older. The main reason for Carlota's move to Bilbao was to make the most of her education, and this has certainly proved successful as she now works as a lawyer. If she had stayed in Galicia it would have been much harder for her to succeed in her chosen career. In contrast, for Joar leaving home at age 16 was very much the start of his 'transition' out of the parental home. Moreover, moving away at 16 was not associated with career aspirations, but that there was simply no choice where he lived.

Joar's and Carlota's experiences provide examples of how families adopt very different strategies to help young people. In general we find in Norway parental support is more likely to be strategic and can involve considerable financial commitment, while in Spain support is more likely to involve more day-to-day exchanges and practices. As such support in Spain is often facilitated either though co-residence or propinquity, whereas in Norway it is more acceptable for parents to provide support at a distance. Among the Norwegian parents that we spoke to, many had made quite a substantial contribution towards their children's new home, or expected to in the future. Some parents contributed to the deposit; others made a contribution to mortgage interest payments, and a family member had to act as guarantor for the mortgage for almost all young Norwegians who had left and bought a house.

In Norway, parents are clearly providing economic capital, but at the same time support is more than about money. What matters is the way that support is provided and what parents 'expect' their children to learn from this. The 'correct' practices of many of our Norwegian respondents' habitus are not just about economic exchanges but about achieving a desired outcome for their children. Parents judge the success of what they do for children not just in terms of financial outcomes but by how they judge they learn the necessary skills to successfully negotiate transitions to independence and adulthood. For example, Felipe and Marta's approach, discussed above, would not thought be out of place in Norway where the importance of learning about responsibility was emphasized by many parents. Norwegian parents were more concerned about spoiling children:

> but we would of course not be those kind of parents whose main concern is to help at all costs, we wouldn't want to spoil our kids so to speak . . . but we do know that loans are tough to manage for young people nowadays . . . I think that it is important that your children do not get the impression that they can do whatever they want without having to take any consequences into account, because they know from previous experiences that their parents will help them out at any cost so to speak . . . Then you might get children who are never able to sort things out, plus not being able also you know, to make well thought-out decisions. [Klara T P F LH]

A couple of parents referred to this attitude that parents should not spoil their children as 'not sewing pillows under their arms'. This is not to say though that by encouraging and expecting young people to 'stand on their own two feet', that family relationships were not important. In fact relationships are key to this process as parental support is based on reciprocity in that parents help out financially but children are expected to act sensibly in return.

As in Bilbao, not all parents in Trondheim have the same attitude to supporting young people and some reject the model of not 'sewing pillows', but rather recognize that it can be parents' prerogative to spoil their children. Anna is a lone mother who has, as she admits, a very close and 'dependent' relationship with her daughter. Yet this closeness does not necessarily mean that she is willing to do the Norwegian thing and provide her daughter with a downpayment with her flat (although she did contribute to refurbishment of the bathroom). Rather she prefers to be there for the nicer things in life:

Interviewer: What is your opinion regarding parents having to help them [adult children]?
Anna: I think it is totally wrong, yes I do think so . . . You should not help because then you have to deal with them not managing on their own, you should help them with matters you find agreeable actually . . . [Anna T P F LH]

Anna describes how she has spent money taking her daughter to Thailand on holiday. She does not think it her duty to help out if her daughter struggles on her own but is quite willing to spend a large amount of money taking her daughter on holiday.

The Norwegian and Spanish families provide an intriguing perspective on parental support and the appropriateness of cultural stereotypes. The interview material confirms that attitudes to parental support *are* different, although in practice what parents *do* does not necessary follow the expected patterns, particularly as we find many Norwegians making considerable financial contributions to their children (this will reflect the overall greater prosperity of the Norwegian families).

How then do our Liverpool families fit in to these models of family support? Relationships between parents and children in Liverpool are more varied and less predictable than either Bilbao or Trondheim. There is more uncertainty in Liverpool about the appropriateness of support. This contrasts with the dominant views in Bilbao where support was almost unquestioned, and in Trondheim where it is recognized as a way of helping out, but reciprocated by young people acting in a responsible manner. In Liverpool there is less acceptance of the idea that parents *should* help and in part this is influenced by discourses of negative connotations of dependency against an ideal that it is best to get by without help. For most respondents in Liverpool, support was negotiated under the auspices of wanting to 'stand on your own feet' and as such was something to contemplate as a last resort, as Marc describes:

> I wouldn't. It wouldn't – I don't – it wouldn't cross my mind to say, look, I'm a hundred pound out, can I borrow it? I'd just say – I'd just wait that little bit longer. OK, if it was a dream house and it was – I had like twelve hours or something to scrape up a hundred pound, then yes, I would ask. But in a normal situation, then I'd just wait the extra month, the extra two months, the extra week longer, I'd just wait. [Marc L 22 M LWP]

Marc associates support with 'handouts' and this differs subtly from the practices in Trondheim, where support was often more proactive and not necessarily restricted to young people in financial difficulties, but was seen more as a 'help up'. We do not want to suggest that Marc's attitude was typical of Liverpool only and in all three cities (including Bilbao) young people were ambivalent about relying, or being seen to rely, on parents (Luescher and Pillemer, 1998; Holdsworth, 2004). The moral value of getting by on one's own was recognized by many respondents. For example, Andrea describes the advantages of 'standing on her own two feet':

> I have that many friends who have left home and where their parents have helped them out a little bit, paying a little and so on . . . But I actually think it is ok, because I then get to prove that I'm able to manage on my own you know . . . It is my apartment. It is me who does everything. [Andrea T 27 F LH]

However, what is distinctive about Liverpool is that there is less sense of what parents *ought* to do. In fact notions of negotiation and contingency are more prevalent in Liverpool and 'it depends' is a common response to questions about whether and how parents should support young people. As part of this many parents reflect on what should *not* be done, and that, sometimes, good intentions can backfire. Wendy is a mother from Liverpool who works as a nursery nurse married to an electrician, and she and her husband have had difficulties dealing with her son's debts:

> So to find out about any further debt, you know. And erm, but I did find out about that again. And erm, I actually, the second time around, we were helping him pay them off and then when I found out about this I said to him, right, I gave him an ultimatum, I said, you know, cut up these cards, right now, or you find somewhere else to live. But I thought it was really out of hand. And it was like, in a

way it was like a slap in the face, 'cos he'd obviously gone and done this after us thinking we'd sorted the first lot of debts out. And he knew that we'd kind of taken them on to give him a start again, so it was like a real slap in the face. You know. And it was quite hurtful really. [Wendy L P F LWP]

Wendy expected her son to recognize that the help his parents gave him was not unconditional, and felt hurt that he did not recognize this. Wendy's experience is fairly typical of other Liverpool parents in that support is often offered in response to a crisis, not as something that is routinely provided. This does reflect the class position of many Liverpool respondents, as there are more working-class families in Liverpool than Trondheim (less so Bilbao). For many Liverpool families the Trondheim model of proactive financial assistance is not feasible. But it also illustrates an essential characteristic of family life in Britain that such assistance is contingent and negotiated from situation to situation. The fact that it is harder to establish a 'British model' of support is precisely because the dominant characteristic is one of contingency. The habitus of many British respondents is one that is essentially open to negotiation; there are less clear ideals of 'correct' practices. In our interviews Liverpool parents sometimes engaged in conversations with the interviewer as to what she thought about appropriate forms of support, reflecting a sense of uncertainty, but also a need for reassurance that 'their' solution was 'correct'. We may reflect that it is perhaps not coincidental that the literature on negotiation and family obligations has emerged mainly from British empirical research.

The emphasis on negotiation of support would suggest that support is more likely to be dependent on good relationships that allow for this processes of negotiation to take place. However, this is not necessarily the case, as Amber's account describes:

Interviewer: OK. And erm, so did you have any like, how did you manage to finance yourself?

Amber: Erm, I was working in erm, St Georges Hotel. Doing that, erm . . . but erm, I got income support[1] and I also got most of me rent paid, in fact I think I got all of it paid then.

Interviewer: Housing benefit?[2]

Amber: Yeah. I mean, it took a while to come through, but eventually they started paying it. And erm, in the end, me Mum ended up lending me the money 'cos we had this huge row when I left, and, 'cos it was a

---

[1] Income support is a means-tested benefit available to UK residents aged between 16 and 60 who are on a low income and either not working, or working less than 16 hours a week.

[2] Housing benefit is a benefit paid to those on a low income who are paying rent. There are special rules for single young people under 25, which restrict the amount of benefit they can receive.

case of me grabbing me stuff in bin bags. Me sister grabbing hold of me and giving me what for (laughs) and, erm, but in the end it was me Mum who lent me some money to pay me first lot of rent until it got paid. Because I wasn't going to go home; she knew that and, so she didn't want me on the streets, so . . .
Interviewer: Mmm. So she helped you. [Amber L 22 F LH]

Amber's mum helped her out not because she agreed with her daughter leaving home, but because if she did not Amber's fate would be far worse. This is one example where the ideal of negotiation is not appropriate; support is not conditional but is about crisis management. Negotiation on the other hand is only feasible where there are viable alternatives and if parents do not have the resources to support adult children there will be less room for negotiation. Negotiation of financial support in particular may be viewed as a middle-class privilege. As Eric, a father of two children, observes, it is possible to support children if both parents are in employment:

> erm I don't resent the money while you know, two of us are working and we can do it. Erm, they were also left some money by a friend of my wife's, who died. And so it's not only our money, its also that money that hopefully I can stretch so far to pay for it. [Eric L P M LH]

In all three locations parents recognized that the amount of support that they could be expected to provide should not be more than they could afford to give. In Liverpool this sense of affordability was strongly influenced by the fact that parents' financial obligations to their children had been extended, particularly for higher education. At the time of the interviews up-front flat-rate tuition fees had been introduced. The amount payable was assessed on parental income and if fees were paid they were usually, but not always, paid by parents. Not all respondents accepted the expectation of parental support that this model of higher education funding assumed.

We need to recognize how the kinds of support that are provided, and why, are contingent on class position (which is, of course, central to Bourdieu's argument about maintenance of social inequalities). In Norway differences by class are less clear, reflecting the fact that there are fewer social inequalities among the families in our sample, which in part reflects the greater social homogeneity in Norwegian society. It is easier, among our respondents, to identify a collective Trondheim habitus that relates support to specific desirable outcomes. In Liverpool the ideal of parental support, which facilitates young people's transition to adulthood through providing financial support, but also through helping young people learn about how to act, is more clearly articulated among middle-class families (see also Allatt and Yeandle, 1992). In working-class families parents may either be unwilling or unable to support (Jones, 1995), and as such are less able to think strategically about the outcomes that they want for their children. Amber's experiences are a case in point, for her relationship with her mother is more about crisis management than learning about responsibility. In Spain, class differences do emerge in how much support young people receive, and in particular there are big contrasts among those living at home, some who have their own bedroom, sitting room and access to car, while others live in more confined spaces and have less access to family resources.

Inter-generational flows

Provision of support within families is not restricted to the kinds of assistance that parents provide for children. We might more commonly think about inter-generational support over the life-course, with older children supporting elderly parents (Kohli, 1999), but reciprocities between generations are far more fluid than this and we should not ignore the possibility that young people contribute to parental household resources. This might involve more direct measures, such as payments for board and lodgings, although in most of the cases where this occurred in our families this was more a symbolic amount, rather than a 'full' contribution. As Felipe and Marta's experience above illustrates, if parents do attempt to make young people pay their way in full this is not necessarily accepted by young people themselves. However, some young people had no option but to financially support their parents. For example, Nacho [B 28 M LH] worked in a bar to actively support his widowed mother. The fact that he took primary responsibility for supporting himself and his widowed mother had a profound impact on his relationship with his mother:

> I had been . . . I had been a little like the man of the house and my mother . . . I was her son, but you see, I was accepted as the man of the house . . . whatever decision that was taken was thought about by both of us but I took the initiative to be a person with initiative and my mother trusts me totally and she knows that I was not going to make a mistake.

In other cases, children might be called upon in an emergency. For example Lydia, a mother in Liverpool, acknowledged how her daughter helped her out if she was short of cash to pay the bills.

Other adult children provide more practical support, often looking after younger brothers and sisters. Children's assistance is strongly associated with a moral judgement and they are recognized as being 'good' in helping their parents out in this way. However, children do not necessarily make the same kinds of judgements of parents. That is we might identify with the moral notion of the 'good' son or daughter as someone who looks after their parents, but parental support for children does not necessarily attract the same kind of judgement. Parental support is considered more as what being a parent is all about, though parents who do not help out may be criticized for this.

Parental advice

It is undoubtedly the case that the financial assistance that parents can provide can make a big impact on young people's ability to leave home, and on their experiences of leaving home, but this is not the only means by which parents play a role. For many young people help and advice are as important as material support. There are a number of different ways in which parental advice may be given and accepted. One approach is the model of preparation that parents should get their children ready for the life in front of them: 'But this was something that I felt faced no problem for me because of the good training that I had received from home you know . . . My parents had prepared me well' [laughter] [Anne Bente, T 25 F LH].

The ideal of preparation suggests a rather static relationship, of children going out in the world and not necessarily coming back. It does not necessarily fit with our approach that stresses the non-linearity of young people's lives. From this perspective a more dynamic relational approach is more appropriate, with parents continuing to be part of young people's lives, although whether they are, and how, are subject to negotiation. To some extent age is a relevant factor here, with the idea of preparation more closely associated with younger ages, around the time of school/work/university transitions. Moreover, as with support, parents' advice is not something that is automatically sought or accepted. This ambivalence is common both among parents and young people, with a strong sense that young people should not replicate their parents' lives. The following exchange is between two Liverpool parents who reflected at length in their interview as to how, and if, they were able to have an impact on their son's life:

> Paul: I think we're more influence now than when he was younger. He's actually said to me, erm, this was a couple of years ago, he said erm, you know when you were younger and your parents give you advice, you think, oh they don't know anything. But as you get a bit older and you realize you didn't take their advice, and things happened the way they said they would, but perhaps they're not quite as dense as you thought. And erm, so, I think he does now er, take advice he might not take all your advice . . .
>
> Elaine: I would much rather have him knowing his own mind, if you like, but I feel that I have to give my, er when I say that I have to give my

voice here, I have to as a parent, going back to being a parent, I feel that I have to give him my advice. I don't always want him to take it. But erm, he will do what he wants to do, and that's OK. But, as a parent, I can't see him stumble, fall, be hurt, knowing that I might have prevented that by telling him. [Paul and Elaine, L Ps LH]

For Paul and Elaine parental advice is something that their son has to want for himself. It is important that he asks for it. But asking for advice needs to be balanced by a strong sense of 'knowing his own mind'. It is acceptable to ask, but not necessarily to act on this advice. This sense of wanting young people to be their own person fits with the notion of youth as a time of becoming and the recognition of learning from one's own mistakes. However not all parents are as reflective as Paul and Elaine and some lament the decline of the 'patriarch' and the lack of respect that young people have for their parents and their opinions.

That parents may want the same for their children is often something that young people will resist, particularly if it represents a narrow set of options and geographical locations. There is often a generational difference in how risks are conceptualized; young people are increasingly being socialized into accepting risks, and this can clash with parents' worldviews that do not so easily accommodate risk. Chris describes how he has to resist his father's view that he should follow in his footsteps:

Well that was one of the reasons, me dad years ago, was putting pressure on me, saying 'you've got to have a job. I can get you in Fords.' And I didn't want to go there. I wanted to have a job I like. And he said 'but it's money'. I said, 'It's not about money.' I said, 'it's about being happy in your job', and that's what I wanted. You know what I mean, 'cos then that's one stress out of life, I don't want to work just to pay the bills, you know what I mean. [Chris L 29 M LH]

Yet while young people such as Chris may find it problematic to accept their parents' viewpoint, and resist their interpretations of what is best for them, the fact that generations may have differing view does not necessarily lead to conflict. As one Spanish father describes, he has learnt from his son's experiences:

no, his life, their lives. That's to say, I've accepted them, and I say I with some reservation. In the last few years my son is one of the people from whom I've learnt a lot, and what have I learnt? To be tolerant, and to be tolerant does not mean . . . I mean, to be tolerant with them but assuming that there are things I don't like; That's to say, one [of my sons] is 24 years old and the other is 23 years old, and they do things that I'm not in agreement with, you see? But at the same time I understand that it is their life so, go ahead. And therefore, once I've begun to understand this . . . [Gotzon, B P M LWP]

Gotzon's account provides an illustration of how it is not just young people who are changing through the process of growing up, and as such engaged in an active construction of habitus, but that these processes are potentially always going on throughout the life-course.

Other family members

The previous section has focused chiefly on parents and parental support and, undoubtedly, these are the most significant 'others' in the leaving-home process. However, our research has highlighted the importance of other family members – chiefly, although not exclusively, siblings.

The importance of siblings is less in terms of any practical help that they might provide in the leaving process but more in terms as being part of the background against which leaving home takes place. In several cases, siblings become important after the leaving-home process has taken place and there are several familiar stories of conflicting relationships at home turning into supportive and pleasurable exchanges once one sibling has left home. Kjell [T 25 M LAH] reports a good relationship with his sister after she had left. They were, he argued, 'too similar and stubborn' when they were under the same roof, but now they meet each other much more often and enjoy each other's company. Jane [L 20 F LH] has one younger brother just about to leave boarding school. Now they do not argue so much and 'I can talk to him for ages'.

There are relatively few examples of older siblings who leave home serving as a role model to their younger brothers or sister and in fact, in several cases, this is explicitly denied. There was at least one case of a home leaver claiming that a brother was the main reason for leaving and in several more cases we gain an insight into the complex family dynamics that constitute part of the domestic background. Matthew [L 24 M LH] felt that his older sister was looking after him (in an almost maternal way) even when he was quite old. In addition she objected to his playing the guitar. Simon [L 21 M LAH] had a sister who was living at home with her small baby. When she left he reports missing looking after the baby and their shared presence in the house. But he also notes that he took his sister for granted and found himself doing more domestic tasks after she left. But siblings are important in that they provide some kind of standard of comparison even if they do not serve as role models directly. Ally [L 21 F LAH] feels that her sister (who went away to a university some distance from home) is more independent than she is. This sense of comparison also applies to the parents. One Norwegian mother of a young mother [T 20 F LH] found herself comparing the two sisters, feeling that the older one (who also became a mother at the age of 20) in some ways prepared her for this more recent departure.

The role of siblings has been under-explored in family sociology generally and our research has highlighted numerous complex stories that deserve telling and further analysis.

Much the same can be said about other family members, in most cases living in a separate household. Grandparents and parents' siblings clearly form part of the background of significant others against which the leaving home process takes place. There are examples of uncles providing the loan of a car or in helping out in the leaving home process or, in Norway, of grandparents acting as guarantors for a loan. In this case [Andrea T 27 F LH] this loan was important but so too was the fact that her grandparents and uncle visited her new flat and approved of what she had done. This kind of support is often opportunistic. For example a young Spanish couple were able to leave home by purchasing a house from relatives at a good price. Carlota was able to do so by moving in with relatives. These examples could be multiplied but do not constitute any clear pattern. This is in keeping with the idea that modern-day kinship, while important, has an elective or voluntary character about it (Finch, 1985). The formal terms of the relationship (grandparent, parent's sibling and so on) are less important than the quality of individual relationships and the specificity of individual family histories. For example, Lapsus [B 19 M LH] lived with his grandmother and parents prior to leaving home, yet while he talks in detail about his relationship with his parents he makes no reference to his grandmother in his account of leaving home.

Friends

Leaving home involves family but we should not overlook the importance of friendship. The significance of friendships, not necessarily in opposition to family, but sometimes instead of it, or as well as it, has been one of the recent additions to the study of intimacy (Allan, 1989; Jamieson, 1998; Pahl, 2000; Weeks et al., 2001). Friendship tends to be approached in opposition to family, for example in the influential work by Weeks on families of choice of non-heterosexuals. Friendships are often significant for non-heterosexuals because of the breakdown of their relations with family members. More specifically for young people, Heath and Cleaver (2003) describe the legitimacy of house sharing as an alternative to more conventional 'family' homes, and not necessarily a temporary arrangement. In these circumstances, friends can be seen to be fulfilling the 'role' of the family. Catherine, from the Liverpool sample, describes how she created a new family among her friends:

But it was like everybody, or quite a few people had come from either quite unusual backgrounds, or not so much broken homes, but just been unhappy, and we just found this little family together; it was so lovely and we stayed here over the holidays and we like made our houses lovely and, they were like proper family homes, everybody would come round and say 'Oh, how lovely is your home!' (laughs) So it was like we created our own little family. Erm, and so its really weird, 'cos I was thinking about it before I came and I thought I moved out of my Mum and Dad's house, and, and then I consider moving out of the family home again when I moved into my little flat. [Catherine L 26 F LH]

Catherine acknowledges her friends as family through the emotional support and sense of togetherness that they shared in their house and as such the experience of sharing is essential to her recognition of friends as family. She also recognizes that the friends with whom she lived shared a sense of needing a supportive environment.

However, not all house shares work out as well as Catherine's. For example, Roja, who shares a flat in Bilbao, complains about one of her house-mates, Ramona, precisely because she does not treat the flat like a 'family home':

She's not here at the moment. We have arguments with her; she has this way of thinking about things. That she's, it's that . . . the three of us have the same way of thinking, well, good, we are living together, in our house . . . And she has another way of seeing things no?

The significance of friendship does not always emerge as a substitute for family, but is sometimes an alternative. Friends are often valued because they *are not* family, and provide different types of relations in young people's lives. This is often linked to spatial practices. For example, both Vito [B 28 M LWP] and Iñaki [B 32 M LH] describe how they spend a lot of time with friends outside of the family home, literally in the street, and this is 'their' space, which is quite different from their parental home. Marc [L 22 M LWP] talks about different experiences of going to friends' parents' houses. Sometimes he is welcomed and treated as another family member, while he says he never goes inside other friends' houses, despite the strength of the friendship, as it would not be acceptable to either his friends or their parents.

Very frequently, friends (like siblings in some cases) provide some basis for comparison. In some cases they may constitute role models of a kind: 'certain male friends who really know how to be having a good time, you know . . . and some who are able to think about and act rationally also' [Kjell T 25 M LWP].

Andrea [T 27 F LH] refers to four girls 'who spend a lot of time together'. She was the first to leave home (relatively late for Norway) and wonders whether she would have left home earlier if one of the others had led the way. The important point is that frequently, in terms of age or experience, friends are not exactly at the same stage in life. When Jane [L 20 F LH] went to university she found that she was taking on a kind of parent role in relation to her slightly younger peers. She seemed to have more experience in everyday practical matters such as paying bills. She began to feel ahead of her contemporaries and notes that some of her friends are still treated as children by their parents. Talk of cohorts or convoys can sometimes obscure the very subtle differences within a generation, which can prove to be of considerable importance in shaping an individual's sense of independence or adulthood.

Generalized other

We frequently heard statements such as: 'all my friends . . . after I'd finished college, they – they went straight to university' [Ally L 21 F LWP]. This sounds like a statement about friendship although there is also an element of generalization or abstraction about such statements. This element of abstraction suggests to us that friends, family members and other young people in the community may be important in young people's lives in a more indirect way. To the extent that young people's lives are orientated around transition processes, one way of making sense of where individuals are up to in their lives is by making comparisons with 'others', these others may be friends, family members or 'other' young people in their local or national community. This sense of the 'other' is similar to Mead's concept of the generalized other. Mead (1934: 154) takes the generalized other to refer to the community to which an individual belongs. For Mead (1934: 155) it is not sufficient for individuals to recognize the attitudes of others towards themselves – they also need to take on board 'their attitudes toward the various phases or aspects of the common social activity or set of social undertakings in which, as members of an organized society or social group, they are all engaged.'

The concept of the generalized other is pertinent when considering transitions, as young people are often looking for different anchorage points to guide them through transition processes. As discussed above, this may often be provided directly by friends and family, although it is often more abstractly achieved through a sense of comparison with 'other people'. For example, Lynn, age 35, who is living at home in Liverpool, recognizes how 'others' might make judgements about her choices:

> Erm, I suppose that's a question for other people because I suppose they could say I could have done this, I should have done that, I

should have done the other. But I don't see that anything I could have done would have made any difference to the way I am now. The way I live now.

For Simon, another Liverpool respondent, his sense of 'others' is drawn on recognizing how 'lucky' he has had it:

Simon: You know, I take it for granted things like that [we've got plenty]. But when look at other people, you know, I could never dream of living the way they have to.
Interviewer: You mean in terms of their lives are worse than yours?
Simon: Mmm. Worse. You know . . . We've had it easy compared to some people. You know, and I don't think a lot of people see that but I do. [L 21 M LWP]

The generalized other has to be used loosely. As it pertains more to what others might be doing, rather than a sense of a recognized community norm, it is a useful way of identifying the boundaries of possible behaviour, rather than a sense of normalized practices. As Hilde, a Norwegian respondent, remarks, she does not think that there is 'a certain norm that says that everyone is to leave home . . . I'm not sure whether I feel this to be the case or not.' We suggest that it might be more productive to think of the active process of generalizing, using the raw material of family, friends and neighbourhood, rather than adopting a more strongly normative notion of the 'generalized other'.

State

So far our discussion of connections and social embeddedness has focused on individuals with whom young people have relationships, yet institutions and structures, such as schools, universities and colleges, workplaces and the state, provide an important part of the context of social embeddedness. In this final section we consider how state functions and policies help to determine boundaries for young people, set constraints and limit (or facilitate) opportunities.

In Britain, Jones and Bell (2000) have detailed the inconsistencies in youth policies and the difficulty of defining clearly recognized practices that accord with the different ways that 'youth', 'dependence' and 'independence' are inferred across different policies and branches of government. It is not surprising, therefore, that parents in Liverpool are often uncertain as to what is the appropriate course of action for them to take as regards supporting their children, when they do not receive a clear message from public policy.

Furthermore, many respondents were critical of the unfairness of recent poli
initiatives in England, particularly concerning the introduction of fees f
higher education. One father criticized MPs for pulling up the ladder behin
them in denying free higher education to current younger generation althou
they themselves had benefited from it. Despite the clear sense of injusti
about university tuition fees, there was not an overwhelming sense that t
state had a duty to look after young people. Peter, a middle-class father w
two sons, suggested that 'if the state can look after anybody, they should lc
after the people who can't look after themselves'. Reflecting negative discou
about welfare, state support in England was identified as a last resort, a
something that young people should not expect an automatic right to, as Ja
a Liverpool student from an affluent background, whose experiences we
cussed in Chapter 5, argued:

> I think the government pays out too much anyway . . . Erm,
> I don't, I don't think it's up to the government to provide cou
> housing, because at the end of the day if you decide to move
> decide to leave home, you've got to look after yourself, rather t
> have, you know, the state pay for you. Otherwise you should sta
> home! [laughs] And have your parents look after you. [Jane L 20 F

Discussion of the potential for the state to do more was, not surprisi
most noticeable in Spain, where state support is least generous. It is alm
if young Spanish people and their parents have been reading Esping-And
in the way they identify the countries with more generous welfare su
for young people:

> Yes, I believe that in Holland it could be that, or in Belgium,
> yes that they give you a lot of help and soon you must give it
> or that it is a special type of loan or something like this. He
> course that does not happen. And soon, I know that they throw
> money away in renting, not like here where generally flats are o
> occupied. And then, they begin to work earlier, they study less a
> then, sure, everyone, everyone, goes together and they leave
> earlier, then it is normal that they leave home earlier or quicke
> B 28 F LWP]

Many young people mentioned Holland in this regard, along with l
Belgium and Sweden (but rarely the UK). Yet it is not just the welfare sta
makes a difference; for example Bergante who, through his job, ha
experience of Swedish working practices and family life, recognizes a re
ship between the kinds of jobs that are open to young people an
leaving:

In Sweden it seems that the families also value this . . . that you fly away earlier, and then . . . I think that there is less support [in the parental home] and also you are put in that situation; imagine that you left home here at 18, what would you live on? . . . with the salaries that they pay and the number of jobs here . . . it is practically . . . you see, it seems to me very difficult that . . . anyone could leave home [here] on their wages. There are salaries that are frankly ridiculous. [Bergante B 31 M LWP]

The sense of unfairness among Spanish young people was not just restricted to comparison with other young people elsewhere in Europe, but also with other young people in Spain. For example Pepi, who compared the situation in Spain with that in Holland and Belgium, argued that in País Vasco, a single person without the right contacts would find it almost impossible to gain access to the small number of subsidized houses available in Bilbao:

Yes because now, here, personal contacts work, that we have always known and it is true . . . then they have a preference for young people and I apply [for housing support], but the result is that the people who get it are married or in a couple, sure, that they have two salaries, the majority, and they have access to housing and I'm only one, while I'm single, yet I remain the last person on the list . . . and this doesn't seem fair to me because there are two people to pay for this subsidized housing and I'm only one.

The state in Spain is not therefore recognized as treating young people fairly, when it does intervene, which in itself is not usual.

State support does not feature much in the Norwegian accounts, however this does not mean that young people did not receive social assistance but it was not something that they thought to reflect on. Norwegian young people acknowledge the various forms of assistance they receive, mainly student loans and housing loans, but do not comment on whether this is adequate or not. Welfare support is not subject to the same kind of interrogation as family support but this does not mean that it is preferred to family support. The families that we spoke to would not necessarily concur with populist accounts that associate the expansion of the state in northern Europe with the demise of family values (Popenoe, 1988). Where social assistance and family support perform complementary roles, as is more the case in Norway, there is less perceived antagonism between family and state. In contrast, in Spain, where welfare is challenged through the family and not the state, there is far more awareness of the limitations of existing state provision.

Concluding remarks

In this chapter, in the process of arguing against an over-individualized account of leaving home (see also Molgat, 2002), we have considered the significant others of parents, other family members and friends, the more institutionalized 'other' represented by the state and the idea of the 'generalized other'. In thinking about these themes we have experienced a certain tension in our choice of words. We have occasionally used the term 'social embeddedness' to underline this sense of the 'others' involved in this transition. Yet this metaphor is not without its difficulties. Its dictionary definition – 'fix firmly in a surrounding mass' – suggests too stable and too subordinate a relationship between a part and a whole. The alternatives are not entirely satisfactory, either. 'Social relationships' is probably too vague and 'social connectedness', with its suggestion of ego-centred social networks, is perhaps too individualistic. We experienced a similar tension in considering 'habitus' (perhaps close to 'social embeddedness') and 'social capital' (closer to 'social connectedness').

Rather than worrying overmuch about our choice of terminology it is probably more important to state what it is we are attempting to convey. We wish to underline the fact that leaving home is not simply an individual accomplishment, however much it may be associated with getting 'a place of one's own', attaining independence or becoming an adult. All kinds of 'others' are involved in this process, chiefly, although not exclusively, parents. Further, these relationships should not be understood as uni-directional, in this case from parent to young person. There are complex interactions and exchanges, the nature of which we wish to convey by our use of the term 'negotiation'. Again, these exchanges and negotiations are not in relation to a 'one-off' transition from parental home to new home but are often protracted and extended over a long period of time, often with moves back and forth.

Social embeddedness (or whatever term we wish to use) is at the heart of the dilemmas of youth research. On the one hand, researchers are interested in the significance of young people establishing their own identity. Being young is about rejecting others, be it family, friends (may be less so) or authority figures. The 'storm-and-stress' model of youth has tended to dominate discourses of transitions, with the emphasis on how young people succeed on their own terms to become their own person. For this reason, we often find that young people's attitude towards others is ambivalent. The classic ambivalence of youth being the recognition of the need for support (emotional or economic) against the desire to 'stand on my own two feet'. This ambivalence is rife for negotiation between those who give and receive support (which does not necessarily always mean from parents to children). While negotiation is a key characteristic of connections with others, and of giving and receiving support, it needs to be put into context. Where models of support are more clearly established, as in the case of both Spain and Norway, there is less opportunity for negotiation, particularly in Spain. It is in Britain where the contingency of support is more prevalent.

However, the model of negotiated support does not encompass the full gamut of experiences. For example, support may be resisted, young people may endorse the ideal of standing on one's own two feet, even if practically this is not always possible. Some young people recognize how over-supportive parents could reduce the options open to them, while some parents construct scenarios about the impossibility of leaving home, where young people's only option is to rely on family. There is, however, an important point to consider here: in recognizing the significance of what support can do, we also need to acknowledge what happens to young people when this support is not provided.

8 Conclusion

We began our account of leaving home by discussing why we were first stimulated to research and write about this event and by reflecting on how leaving-home experiences relate to a number of personal, social and political concerns, in addition to theoretical perspectives. Leaving home is one of those intriguing events that everyone 'does' (or most people do) so that it can almost seem to be too self-evident to warrant academic study. Yet as we have explored throughout this book, while leaving home is often regarded as the 'natural thing' to do, what is intriguing about it is how what is 'natural' varies between different contexts. The contexts within which leaving home takes place are, therefore, crucial to understanding young people's experiences of leaving home, and how these correspond to related concerns to do with home, independence and adulthood. Context however, is not something that can necessarily be easily distilled to either a specific spatial or temporal location. For example, despite the clear differences in patterns of leaving home in northern and southern Europe, it is far from straightforward to identify a 'Spanish' or a 'British' context, in the sense that there is a Spanish or a British way of doing things. As we have explored throughout the book, young people negotiate with contexts at differing levels of abstraction including the personal, family as well as the wider community, and also different time frames. Moreover, these negotiations are constructed with reference to other social relations, particularly gender and class.

In this final chapter we seek to draw together these different conceptualizations of context so to give a summary of the main ways in which young people's experiences of leaving home relate to the substantive themes of the book.

Time and generation

We started our account by providing an overview of leaving home transitions in different contexts. As is evident from the discussion of survey data on leaving home, one of the most important characteristics that distinguishes leaving-home transitions in different locations is timing. It is problematic to relate these differences in timing observed at a macro-level to more individualized accounts of leaving home. We found considerable variation in the sequencing of life-course events both within and between countries. In general this would appear to support the claims of 'do-it-yourself' biographies in that most young people made decisions about leaving home/living with parents to suit their circumstances and opportunities. For many young people, leaving home was opportunistic and came about due to a particular set of events and circumstances, rather than young people following a predetermined script. Young people and parents in Spain were also more concerned about leaving home at the 'right time'. In contrast to their Norwegian and British counterparts, this was closely identified with leaving home to get married once transitions out of education and into employment had been successfully negotiated. While the possibility of following alternative routes is acknowledged in Spain (and some young people had chosen to leave home prior to getting married) many parents and young people argued that structural factors, such as lack of suitable housing, and 'cultural' norms about family life, both meant that these 'alternative' transitions are less appropriate in Bilbao.

The views expressed by Spanish young people and parents would suggest that leaving-home transitions have not changed much for the current younger generation. In fact a common interpretation of contemporary Spanish family life is that it is characterized by 'traditional' values and practices. According to some commentators it is, therefore, open to the possibility of change, specifically convergence to north European individualized practices of family life. However, this interpretation does not hold up to close scrutiny as one of the most important themes to emerge from the interviews in all three locations, including Spain, is the emphasis on how much life has changed for the current younger generation. While parents acknowledge that they also left home to marry, albeit at a younger age, their experiences of living with parents and their reasons for leaving were very different. Many parents talked about leaving to 'escape' the parental home and to better themselves. In contrast, their relationships with their own children are said to be good, with many young people and parents describing their relationships as equivalent to those between friends, in contrast to a more 'traditional' authoritarian style of family life. However this sense of freedom and increasing choice for the younger generation must be set against an equally strong sense of increasing economic hardship. Many parents, in particular, expressed concern about how much 'harder' it is for young people nowadays, faced with the rising costs of education, uncertain labour markets and expensive housing.

Home

Leaving home clearly relates to spatial practices and the relationship between the production of space and social relations. We have explored this dimension of leaving home by reflecting on how the transition itself, or the expectation of leaving home, stimulates reflection on meanings of home itself. This raises intriguing issues concerning translation, as while the Norwegian *hjem* is a reasonable translation for the English 'home', the Spanish *casa* does not necessarily suggest the same emotional qualities or elasticity of scale implied by 'home'. Hence while questions about meanings of 'home' often elicited animated responses among the British and Norwegian interviewees, many Spanish respondents found questions about meanings of *casa* rather confusing. However, despite these difficulties in translation, analysis of the transcripts reveals considerable overlaps and similarities between the meanings attached to each. In particular we find a strong sense of positive emotions towards 'home', and an emphasis on 'home' as a place of safety, security and retreat. In unpacking these meanings we explore different conceptions of home spaces: the practical, symbolic and imaginary.

We do not want to suggest that experiences of 'home' are always positive, and some young people talked about very difficult experiences of violence and oppression, from parents, step-parents or partners. In most cases these were women and by far the majority of these came from Liverpool. The relative absence of similar accounts in the Bilbao and Trondheim samples could reflect reality, differences in methods of recruiting respondents, or a greater desire to present a positive view of Norwegian and Spanish family life. It is not possible for us to tell which is the most likely explanation and this is a topic worthy of further research.

Independence

Independence is clearly a key theme of leaving home, but how they correspond is less clear. One of our objectives in writing this book has been to interrogate assumptions linking leaving home and independence, particularly the conventional functional model that assumes that leaving home implies independence and vice versa. In order to move beyond this rather simplistic model of residential transitions and independence, we identified different ways of conceptualizing independence, distinguishing between 'freedom from' or 'freedom to'. The former is more closely associated with residential separation – independence as freedom from parental authority and scrutiny – whereas the latter is less contingent on living arrangements.

Many young people, particularly in Spain, viewed independence as freedom to do what they wanted to do, to think what they wanted and be who they wanted to be. Being independent in this sense has very little to do with establishing an independent residence. The link between autonomy, economic and residential independence was made more strongly by Norwegian and British respondents, as leaving home was recognized as a important demonstration of young people's transition to independence. From the interviews with parents and young people we also gain a strong sense of the role that parents play in helping young people become independent. This often starts in the parental home with parents giving young people the space and opportunity to become independent. However, independence does not emerge as a clearly demarcated state; rather, distinctions between independence and dependence are fluid and inter-changeable and we find it more useful to conceptualize leaving home as a transition between different inter-dependencies than a movement from dependency to independence. For example young people might become more 'dependent' on their parents again if they have children, or dependent on their partners. Finally, some parents acknowledge that they were also dependent on their adult children, either financially or (more frequently) for emotional support. This is more common among divorced or widowed parents.

Adulthood

Discussions of adulthood generate similar issues to those for independence. In fact being an 'adult' may be taken as a definition of independence and vice versa. Yet adulthood is often conceptualized in more abstract or moral terms, but less so than independence, and as such is often treated as a more ambiguous status. 'Adulthood' may be framed in opposition to 'childhood' or 'childlike', yet it is more likely that young people recognize their ability to act as both adults and children. If we try to identify a key concept that defines adulthood in all three contexts, this would be responsibility, both for one's own actions and also for other people. The emphasis on responsibility for others is not necessarily contingent on residential independence. In fact, for some respondents, the opposite is the case as young people who take responsibility for other family members in the parental home and see their caring role as a source of a sense of adulthood. Moreover, not all young people view adulthood in a positive light. Some respondents rejected what they saw as a certain set of values and ways of acting associated with adulthood, that is being 'sensible', having a routine job and everything 'sorted out'. Even respondents who acknowledge themselves as adults, recognize that this was reinforced by their ability to be 'childlike' and forget their responsibilities for a while, be it through playing with their children or relaxing with friends and family.

Connected transitions: significant and generalized others

Leaving home is not a transition that young people experience in isolation. Parents, siblings, grandparents, other family members and friends all play a role in framing the context in which young people experience living at and leaving home, but also more directly through supportive roles. We have discussed how these connections create contexts of leaving home. For example attitudes to parental support clearly impact on how young people are expected to act 'responsibility' in a Norwegian and British context or as manifestations of family solidarity in Spain. Hence in understanding the differences in parental support in particular, it is not so much a question of *how much* support is provide but *how* it is offered, or not, as the case may be.

In Spain parents tend to emphasize children's material wellbeing and there is less concern that family support could be detrimental to young people's sense of independence and responsibility. In Norway, parents are willing to help children, however most are wary about spoiling adult children. Support was endorsed where it could be constructively viewed as a 'help-up', which enables young people to become independent and learn about responsibility. British respondents echoed Norwegian concern about spoiling, however some respondents went further, arguing that the best way to become independent is by young people 'standing on their own two feet', and not to rely on either parents or the state. Support was often given more in response to crisis management, rather than strategic practices. This does not mean to say that respondents were happy with the amount of social assistance available – in fact quite the opposite was true among many Spanish and British respondents, although there is some uncertainty regarding what the state could do to help more.

We also need to recognize that connections with others, both significant and generalized, are also ways of mediating context, for example through comparison with family and friends, or 'the conversations with oneself'. We can see how young people are continually situating their experiences against those of generalized and significant others and how these processes are key to the ways in which a more general sense of context can become embodied and made 'real'.

Knowledge transfer and policy considerations

Leaving home is a personal journey, or collection of journeys, and as such is often portrayed by the parents and young people we spoke to as something that is not necessarily anything to do with the state. In the UK, in particular, debates about welfare dependency have emphasized a narrower concept of support as a handout that deprives recipients of their self-esteem, as they become 'dependent' on the state. Yet this notion that one must stand on one's own two feet, or at least only ask for the support of close kin, is not an ideal that is necessarily appropriate or applicable for all.

Here the Norwegian experiences have been particularly illuminating. The Norwegian approach of treating support as a help up is different from predominantly British concerns about handouts, as support can be seen as a strategic practice that enables young people to learn about responsibility and taking care of themselves and other people. The trade off between help and responsibility that Trondheim families adopt does appear to create less anxiety among family members than the crisis responses that are more characteristic in the Liverpool families. Obviously the Norwegian model is more appropriate for wealthier families with the resources to act strategically and is typical of middle-class British experiences as well as Norwegian ones.

In fact there is increasing evidence of how families are adopting strategies to support young people. For example 'offset' mortgages in the UK are sold to parents and young people as a way for the former to avoid taxes on their savings and for the latter to access to property market. We might speculate that as the 'costs' of housing and education transitions in particular increase in Great Britain, then these kinds of strategies will become more commonplace.

The ways in which families can and do develop strategies of support have implications for youth policies. The recognition of support as a help up rather than a handout is just as applicable to social assistance as it is to family support. There is, in the UK (and England specifically), a sense of injustice and confusion over a range of youth policies but particularly those to do with higher education, where the shifting goalposts of 'who pays' reflect anxieties about parental support. When up-front tuition fees were first introduced, the expectation was that parents would pay, although, as a lot of our parents argued, this expectation was not something that they necessarily agreed with. Current plans for student funding are based on the assumption of students paying after graduation, explicitly to remove the necessity of young people being dependent on parents.

Embedded in debates about the future of higher education funding is a lack of clarity regarding the responsibilities of parents for adult children and *vice versa*, although the pendulum appears to have swung back to the notion that young people should not be dependent on their parents. We came across this uncertainty about the 'right thing to do' so very often in Liverpool and parents often expressed their doubts as well as sought reassurance that they did the best for their children. Maybe it is partly a factor of translation but we did not feel the same sense of uncertainty in Trondheim and Bilbao. In Bilbao the laments about the state are more predictable, with complaints that the state does nothing and needs to do more. Yet these statements are often couched in rather vague terms of reference, with little desire to see the role, and perceived power, of the family diminish and more concern with how the state could intervene to lower prices and make housing more 'affordable'. The policy message is therefore a complex one: ideally leaving home should be a personal journey and not something dictated by outside forces, except for young people whose circumstances demand otherwise (such as the young people in Liverpool who left home via the youth housing project). There was also a need to facilitate this financially, as expressed in Bilbao, or through more joined-up thinking and clarity of guidance, as expressed by many Liverpool parents.

Contexts, transitions, linearity and liminality

Throughout this book, our interest in putting 'transitions in context' has stimulated us to think though how we use these two concepts. In Chapter 2 we mapped out the multiple meanings that can attach to the term 'context'. All of these refer to inclusion within some wider social entity: class, community, welfare regime, state or broader historical current such as 'individualization'. Yet again, as we discussed in relation to the term 'culture', negotiations still take place and we are as concerned with the ways in which our young people and their parents make use of elements from these wider entities as with the ways in which these contextual factors limit or shape choices and decisions. Parental support, for example, cannot therefore be reduced to economic criteria but is given, received, denied or refused as part of strategic practices, that are incorporated into habitus. Thus our discussion of 'the generalized other', sees this not as some rather abstracted entity detached from but influential upon everyday practices but as something that emerges out of everyday practices involving family, friends and other more identifiable individuals or institutions.

Emerging debates in youth research which query the appropriateness of the concept of the linear transition, have influenced our account of transitions. While we would not want to argue for concept abandonment, we recognize the need to think through how the concept of transition can be used in such a way that it does not necessarily mean that we restrict ourselves to linear models, nor that we focus on young people's experiences with reference restricted to orientations between points of departure and destination. It is not the sense of transition or journey that is the problem, as transitions are an essential characteristic of the life-course, including entering partnerships and partnership dissolution, becoming a parent, children leaving home, widowhood and orphanhood. What is important, though, is how we view the relative importance of the spaces and times in between and how these relate to start and end points. Conventionally, youth transitions, particularly in housing, education and employment, did have a clearly identified start and end point but these are now far fuzzier. The complexity of housing and employment careers is clearly evident but, even in education, which might appear more constrained by fixed points of entry and exit, the development of life-long learning is moving in the same direction. Any study of transitions therefore suggests a study of liminality as well. For example, we can see how, in recent years, studies of student's housing, shared professional housing and young people's housing careers have focused attention on 'what goes on in between', and, as Sue Heath argues, are just as relevant as the start and end points. Moreover, the idea that there is a fixed end point to youth transitions is inappropriate: young people might never leave home, they might return home, partnerships might dissolve, individuals might return to university, take a career break or experience redundancy.

The critique of the emphasis on linearity does not just apply to personal accounts. One of our motivations for carrying out our research on leaving home was the sense that leaving home patterns were changing in late modern societies and there was, particularly in northern European and North American societies, a lament that young people were becoming too complacent. In the UK, for example, we encountered numerous articles in the media where older generations of journalists take issue with the apparent failings of youth. Barbara Ellen, writing in the *Observer* (23 November 2003) lamented that

> we must be getting things very wrong if we're turning out a new generation so soppy and spoiled they won't move out of the family home until they can buy their own place – missing out on all those formative years renting doss-holes so cheap and scary you need a rape alarm to walk to your own bathroom.

Ellen's conclusion is that this change is going in the 'wrong' direction. Yet, as we have argued for personal transitions, why should we necessarily look for linear change at a more collective level? While the sense of how things are different now than in the past is very strong, it is not possible to identify in which direction change is going.

The case of Spain is interesting here as so much that was written about the 'new' Spanish family after the death of Franco assumed that the Spanish family would become more northern European. The monitoring of family trends has focused on how the family is becoming more 'modern', in terms of cohabitation, divorce and extra-marital fertility. Yet our observation of change in Spain, and elsewhere, is not of a one-way process towards a modern ideal, but a more complex shifting of practices and expectations between, and also within, generations.

Individualization

Debates about individualization have been very dominant in youth studies
in recent years, particularly in understanding constructions of identities and
how, as Bauman identifies, this has shifted from a 'given' into a 'task'. However, discussions of individualization do not override longstanding debates
about structures but rather are often at the heart of tensions between structure
and agency. Recognizing that 'everyone' has a choice does not mitigate the
need to understand how these choices are made and the decisions that
individuals take. This is particularly relevant for leaving home.

As we have discussed throughout this book, the transition may be treated
as a personal experience – one that is very much dependent on individual
circumstances, with less formal, or institutional guidance than other 'transitions' around education and employment (although the experiences of students leaving or not leaving home is one possible exception). Yet among the
accounts of young people's experiences that we collected, what seems to matter is how the young recognize their sense of 'being in charge' of their own
lives and, crucially, how they recognize their responsibility for their outcomes.
Individualization, we contend, is less to do with the declining importance of
structures, or context from our perspective, but is more relevant in thinking
through how young people experience negotiations with different abstractions
of context and how they recognize their own accountability. From Spanish
young people who are concerned not to upset their families, Norwegian youth
learning about responsibility and British young people negotiating conflicting
messages about parental responsibility; we have seen how their experiences
often involve achieving one's goal in a way that directly involves others, both
significant and generalized, while still maintaining a strong sense of 'choice'.

Bibliography

Aassve, A., Billari, F.C., Mazzuco, S., and Ongaro, F. (2002) Leaving home: a comparative analysis of ECHP, *Journal of European Social Policy*, 12: 259–75.

Adam, B. (1990) *Time and Social Theory*. Cambridge: Polity Press.

Adam, B. (1995) *Timewatch: The Social Analysis of Time*. Cambridge: Polity Press.

Ahmed, S., Casteñeda, C., Fortier, A.-M. and Sheller, M. (eds) (2003) *Uprootings/ Regroundings: Questions of Home and Migration*. Oxford: Berg.

Alanen, L. (1988) Rethinking childhood, *Acta Sociologica*, 31: 53–67.

Allan, G. (1989) *Friendship: Developing a Sociological Perspective*. Brighton: Harvester Wheatsheaf.

Allatt, P. (1997) Conceptualising youth: transitions, risk and the public and the private, in J. Bynner, L. Chisholm and A. Furlong (eds) *Youth, Citizenship and Social Change in a European Context*. Aldershot: Ashgate, pp. 89–102.

Allatt, P. and Yeandle, S. (1992) *Youth Unemployment and the Family*. London: Routledge.

Allen, J. and Pryke, M. (1994) The production of service space, *Environment and Planning D: Society and Space*, 12: 453–75.

Altman, I. and Gauvin, M. (1981) A cross-cultural and dialectic analysis of homes, in L.S. Liben, A.H. Patterson, and N. Newcombe (eds) *Spatial Representation and Behaviour Across the Lifespan*. New York: Academic Press, pp. 283–320.

Anderson, M. (1985) The emergence of the modern life cycle in Britain, *Social History*, 10: 69–87.

Antonucci, T.C. and Akiyama, H. (1995) Convoys of social relations: family and friendships within a life-span context, in R. Blieszner and V.H. Bedford (eds) *Handbook of Ageing and the Family*. New York: Greenwood Press.

Apter, T. (2001) *The Myth of Maturity*. New York: W.W. Norton.

Aquilino, W.S. (1991) Family structure and home-leaving: a further specification of the relationship, *Journal of Marriage and the Family*, 53: 999–1010.

Ariès, P. (1962) *Centuries of Childhood*. London: Jonathan Cape.

Avery, R., Goldscheider, F. and Speare Jr, A. (1992) Feathered nest/gilded cage: parental income and leaving home in the transition to adulthood, *Demography*, 29: 375–88.

Bachelard, G. (1964) *The Poetics of Space*. New York: The Orion Press.

Backett, K.C. (1982) *Mothers and Fathers: A Study of the Development and Negotiation of Parental Behaviour*. London: Macmillan.

Baizán. P., Michielin, F. and Billari. F. (2002) Political economy and life-course patterns: the heterogeneity of occupational, family and household trajectories of young Spaniards, *Demographic Research*, 6(8): 191–240.

Bauman, Z. (2002) Preface, in U. Beck and E. Beck-Gernsheim (eds) *Individualization: Institutionalized Individualism and its Social and Political Consequences*. London: Sage.

Beck, U. and Beck-Gernsheim, E. (1995) *The Normal Chaos of Love*. London: Polity Press.

Beck, U. and Beck-Gernsheim, E. (2002) *Individualization: Institutionalized Individualism and its Social and Political Consequences*. London: Sage.

Berlin, I. (2002) *Liberty: Incorporating Four Essays on Liberty*, edited by Henry Hardy. Oxford: Oxford University Press.

Bernardes, J. (1998) *Family Studies: An Introduction*. London: Routledge.

Berne, E. (1968) *Games People Play: The Psychology of Human Relationships*. Harmondsworth: Penguin.

Berrington, A. and Murphy, M. (1994) Changes in the living arrangements of young adults in Britain during the 1980s, *European Sociological Review*, 10: 253–7.

Bestard Camps, J. and Contreras Hernández, J. (1997) Family, kinship and residence in urban Catalonia: the modernity of 'Pairalism', in M. Gullestad and M. Segalen (eds) *Family and Kinship in Europe*. London: Pinter, pp. 31–46.

Billari, F.C. (2001) The analysis of early life-courses: complex descriptions of the transition to adulthood, *Journal of Population Research*, 18: 119–42.

Billari, F.C. and Micheli, G.A. (2001) Social norms on agents' demographic events. Preliminaries for a (multi-) agent-based approach, in R. Conte and C. Dellarocas (eds), *Social Order in Multiagent Systems*. Dordrecht: Kluwer, pp. 201–21.

Billari, F.C., Philipov, D. and Baizán Muñoz, P. (2001) Leaving home in Europe: The experience of cohorts born around 1960, *International Journal of Population Geography*, 7: 311–38.

Birdwell-Pheasant, D. and Lawrence-Zúniga, D. (eds) (1999) *House Life: Space, Place and Family in Europe*. Oxford: Berg.

Blum, V. and Nast, H. (1996) Where's the difference? The heterosexualization of alterity, in H. Lefebvre and J. Lacan, *Environment and Planning D: Society and Space*, 14: 559–80.

Bourdieu, P. (1990) *The Logic of Practice*. Stanford: Stanford California Press.

Bourdieu, P. (1997) The forms of capital, in A.H. Halsey, H. Lauder, P. Brown and A. Stuart Wells (eds) *Education, Culture, Economy and Society*. Oxford: Oxford University Press.

Bourdieu, P. and Passeron, J.-C. (1977) *Reproduction in Education, Society and Culture*. London: Sage.

Brannen, J., Heptinstall, E. and Bhopal, K. (2000) *Connecting Children: Care and Family Life in Later Childhood*. London: Routledge/Falmer.

Brannen, J. and Nilsen, A. (2002) Young people's time perspectives: from youth to adulthood, *Sociology*, 36: 513–37.

Brannen, J. and O'Brien, M. (eds) (1996) *Children in Families: Research and Policies.* London: Falmer.

Breen, R. and Goldthorpe, J.H. (2001) Class mobility and merit: the experience of two British birth cohorts, *European Sociological Review*, 17: 81–102.

Budak, M.-A., Liaw, K.-L., Kwabe, H. (1996) Co-residence of household heads with parents in Japan: a multivariate explanation, *International Journal of Population Geography*, 2: 133–52.

Bynner, J. (2001) British youth transitions in comparative perspective, *Journal of Youth Studies*, 4: 5–23.

Bynner, J., Chisholm, L. and Furlong, A. (1997) A new agenda for youth research, in J. Bynner, L. Chisholm and A. Furlong (eds) *Youth, Citizenship and Social Change in a European Context*. Aldershot: Ashgate, pp. 3–14.

Bynner, J., Elias, P., McKnight, A., Pan, H. and Pierre, G. (2002) *Young People's Changing Routes to Independence*. York: Joseph Rowntree Foundation.

Castells, M. (1997) *The Power of Identity* (Volume 2 of *The Information Age: Economy, Society and Culture*). Oxford: Blackwell.

Cavalli, A. and Galland, O. (1995) *Youth in Europe*. London: Pinter.

Chapman, T. (1999) Spoiled home identities: the experience of burglary, in T. Chapman and J. Hockey (eds) *Ideal Homes? Social Change and Domestic Life*. London: Routledge, pp. 133–46.

Cieslik, M. and G. Pollock (eds) (2002) *Young People in Risk Society*. Aldershot: Ashgate.

Cohen, P. and Ainley, P. (2000) In the country of the blind? Youth studies and cultural studies in Britain, *Journal of Youth Studies*, 3: 79–95.

Cordón, J. (1997) Youth residential independence and autonomy: a comparative study, *Journal of Family Issues*, 18(6): 576–607.

Corijn, M. and Klijzing. E. (eds) (2000) *Transitions to Adulthood in Europe*. Dordrecht: Kluwer Academic Publishers.

Cowan, P.A. (1991) Individual and family life transitions: a proposal for a new definition, in P.A. Cowan and M. Hetherington (eds) *Family Transitions*. Hillsdale, NJ: Lawrence Erlbaum.

Crossley, N. (2001) The phenomenological habitus and its construction, *Theory and Society*, 30: 81–120.

De Jong Gierveld, J., Liefbroer, A.C. and Beekink, E. (1991) The effect of parental resources on patterns of leaving home among young adults in the Netherlands, *European Sociological Review*, 7: 55–71.

De Vos, S. (1989) Leaving the parental home: patterns in six Latin American countries, *Journal of Marriage and the Family*, 51: 615–26.

Després, C. (1991) The meaning of home: literature review and directions for future research and theoretical development, *Journal of Architectural and Planning Research*, 8: 96–115.

Douglas, M. (1991) The idea of home: a kind of space, *Social Research*, 58: 287–307.

Douglass, W. (1988) The Basque stem family household: myth or reality? *Journal of Family History*, 13: 75–89.

Duncan, S. and Edwards, R. (1999) *Lone Mothers: Gendered Moral Rationalities*. Basingstoke: Macmillan.

Dunne, G. (1998) 'Pioneers behind our own front doors': new models for the organization of work in partnerships, *Work, Employment and Society*, 12: 277–95.

Edmunds, J. and Turner, B. (2002) *Generations, Culture and Society*. Buckingham: Open University Press.

EGRIS (2001) Misleading trajectories: transition dilemmas of young adults in Europe, *Journal of Youth Studies*, 4: 101–18.

Elder, G.H. (1978) Approaches to social change and the family, in J. Demos and S.S. Boocock (eds) *Turning Points: Historical and Sociological Essays on the Family*. Chicago: University of Chicago Press.

Esping-Andersen, G. (1999) *Social Foundations of Post-Industrial Economies*. Oxford: Oxford University Press.

Eurostat (2002) *ECHP UDP Manual*, Reference no. Doc.Pan 168/2002–12. Luxembourg: Eurostat.

Evans, K. and Furlong, A. (1997) Metaphors of youth transitions: niches, pathways, trajectories or navigations, in J. Bynner, L. Chisholm and A. Furlong (eds) *Youth, Citizenship and Social Change in a European Context*. Aldershot: Ashgate, pp. 17–41.

Fernández Cordón, J.-A. (1997) Youth residential independence and autonomy: a comparative study, *Journal of Family Issues*, 6: 572–607.

Finch, J. (1989) *Family Obligations and Social Change*. Cambridge: Polity Press.

Finch, J. and Mason, J. (1993) *Negotiating Family Responsibilities*. London: Routledge.

Flatau, P., James, I., Watson, R., Wood, G. and Hendershott, P. (2003) *Leaving the parental home in Australia over the twentieth century: Evidence from the household income and labour dynamics in Australia survey*. Paper presented at HILDA conference, Melbourne.

Fog Olwig, K. (1999) Travelling makes a home: mobility and identity among West Indians, in T. Chapman and J. Hockey (eds) *Ideal Homes? Social Change and Domestic Life*. London: Routledge, pp. 73–83.

Ford, J., Rugg, J. and Burrows, R. (2002) Conceptualising the contemporary role of housing in the transition to adult life in England, *Urban Studies*, 39: 2455–567.

Fortier, A.-M. (2003) Making home: queer migrations and motions of attachment, in S. Ahmed, C. Casteñeda, A.-M. Fortier and M. Sheller (eds) *Uprootings/ Regroundings: Questions of Home and Migration*. Oxford: Berg, pp. 115–36.

Fraser, N. and Gordon, L. (1994) 'Dependency' demystified: inscriptions of power in a keyword of the welfare state, *Social Politics*, Spring: 4–31.

Furlong, A. and Cartmel, F. (1997) *Young People and Social Change: Individualization and Risk in Late Modernity*. Buckingham: Open University Press.

Geertz, C. (1973) *The Interpretation of Cultures*. London: Hutchinson.

Gillies, V. (2000) Young people and family life: analysing and comparing disciplinary discourses, *Journal of Youth Studies*, 3: 211–28.

Gluckman, M. (ed.) (1964) *Closed Systems and Open Minds: The Limits of Naivety in Social Anthropology*. Edinburgh and London: Oliver & Boyd.

Goldscheider, F.K. and DaVanzo, J. (1989) Pathways to independent living in early adulthood: marriage, semiautonomy and premarital residential independence, *Demography*, 26: 597–614.

Goldscheider, F.K. and Goldscheider, C. (1999) *The Changing Transition to Adulthood*. London: Sage.

Goldscheider, F.K., Thornton, A. and Yang, L.S. (2001) Helping out the kids: expectations about parental support in young adulthood, *Journal of Marriage and the Family*, 63: 727–40.

Goldscheider, F.K., Thornton, A. and Young-DeMarco, L. (1993) A portrait of nest-leaving process in early adulthood, *Demography*, 30: 683–99.

Gouldner, A.W. (1970) *The Coming Crisis of Western Sociology*. London: Heinemann.

Greenhalgh, S. (1988) Fertility as mobility: sinic transitions, *Population and Development Review*, 14: 629–74.

Greenhalgh, S. (1990) Towards a political economy of fertility: anthropological contributions, *Population and Development Review*, 16: 85–106.

Gullestad, M. (1992) *The Art of Social Relations: Essays on Culture, Social Action and Everyday Life in Modern Norway*. Oslo: Scandinavian University Press.

Gurney, G.M. (1997) '. . . Half of me was satisfied': making sense of home through episodic ethnographies, *Women's Studies International Forum*, 20: 373–86.

Gutmann, M., Pullum-Piñón, S.M. and Pullum, T.W. (2002) Three eras of young adult home leaving in twentieth-century America, *Journal of Social History*, 35: 533–76.

Hajnal, J. (1965) European marriage patterns in perspective, in D.V. Glass and D.E.C. Eversley (eds) *Population in History: Essays in Historical Demography*. London: Arnold.

Haley, J. (1980) *Leaving Home*. New York: McGraw Hill.

Hall, S. and Jefferson, T. (eds) (1997) *Resistance Through Rituals: Youth Subcultures in Post-War Britain*. London: Hutchinson in association with the Centre for Contemporary Cultural Studies.

Hammel, E.A. (1990) A theory of culture for demography, *Population and Development Review*, 16: 455–86.

Hareven, T.K. (1991) The home and the family in historical perspective, *Social Research*, 58: 253–85.

Harvey, D. (1989) *The Condition of Postmodernity*. Oxford: Basil Blackwell.

Hayward, G. (1975) Home as an environmental and psychological concept, *Landscape*, 20: 2–9.

Heath, S. and Cleaver, E. (2003) *Young, Free and Single: Twenty-Somethings and Household Change*. Basingstoke: Palgrave Macmillan.

Hockey, J. (1999) The ideal of home: domesticating the institutional space of old age and death, in T. Chapman and J. Hockey (eds) *Ideal Homes? Social Change and Domestic Life*. London: Routledge, pp. 108–18.

Hockey, J. and James, A. (2003) *Social Identities Across the Life-Course*. Basingstoke: Palgrave Macmillan.

Holdsworth, C. (2000) Leaving home in Great Britain and Spain, *European Sociological Review*, 16: 201–22.

Holdsworth, C. (2004) Family support during the transition out of the parental home in Britain, Spain and Norway, *Sociology*, 38: 909–26.

Holdsworth, C. and Elliott, J. (2001) The timing of family formation in Britain and Spain, *Sociological Research Online*, 6 (2). See http://www.socresonline.org.uk/6/2/holdsworth.html.

Holdsworth, C. and Irazoqui Solda, M. (2002) First housing moves in Spain: An analysis of leaving home and first housing acquisition, *European Journal of Population*, 18: 1–19.

Holdsworth, C. and Patiniotis, J. (2004) The choices and experiences of higher education students living in the parental report, *Final Report to Economic and Research Council*, Award number: R000223985. See http://www.regard.ac.uk/research-findings/R000223985/report.pdf.

Holdsworth, C., Voas, D. and Tranmer, M. (2002) Leaving home in Spain: when, where and how, *Regional Studies*, 36: 989–1004.

House of Commons Health Committee (2004) *Obesity: Third Report of Session 2003–04*, Volume I. London: The Stationery Office.

Hunt, P. (1989) Gender and the construction of home life, in G. Allan and G. Crow (eds) *Home and Family: Creating the Domestic Sphere*. Macmillan: Basingstoke, pp. 66–81.

Hutson, S. and Jenkins, R. (1989) *Taking the Strain: Families, Unemployment and the Transition to Adulthood*. Milton Keynes: Open University Press.

Iacovou, M. and Berthoud, R. (2001) *Young People's Lives: A Map of Europe*. Colchester: Institute for Social and Economic Research.

Irwin, S. (1995) *Rights of Passage: Social Change and the Transition from Youth to Adulthood*. London: UCL Press.

James, A. and Prout, A. (eds) (1997) *Constructing and Reconstructing Childhood*, 2nd edn. London: Falmer Press.

James, A., Jenks, C. and Prout, A. (1998) *Theorizing Childhood*. Cambridge: Polity Press.

Jamieson, L. (1998) *Intimacy: Personal Relationships in Modern Society*. Cambridge: Polity Press.

Jamieson, L. (1999) Intimacy transformed: a critical look at the pure relationship, *Sociology*, 33: 477–94.

Jenks, C. (ed.) (1982) *The Sociology of Childhood: Essential Readings*. London: Batsford.

Johnson, R.W. and DaVanzo, J. (1998) Economic and cultural influences on the decision to leave home in Peninsular Malaysia, *Demography*, 35: 97–114.

Jones, G. (1995) *Leaving Home*. Buckingham: Open University Press.

Jones, G. and Bell, R. (2000) *Balancing Acts: Youth, Parenting and Public Policy*. York: Joseph Rowntree Trust.

Jones, G. and Martin, G. (2003) The parenting of youth: social protection and economic dependence. *Final Report to Economic and Social Research Council*, Award Number: *ESRC R00023837*. See http://www.regard.ac.uk/research-findings/R000238379/report.pdf.

Jones, G. and Wallace, C. (1992) *Youth, Family and Citizenship*. Buckingham: Open University Press.

Jonsson, J.O. (2001) Towards a post-Fordist life-course regime? Generational changes in transitions and volatility, in J. O. Jonsson and C. Mills (eds) *Cradle to Grave: Life-Course Change in Modern Sweden*. Durham: SociologyPress.

Jurado Guerrero, T. (2001) *Youth in Transition: Housing, Employment, Social Policies and Families in France and Spain*. Aldershot: Ashgate.

Jurado Guerrero, T. and Naldini, M. (1997) Is the South so different? Italian and Spanish families in comparative perspective, *South European Society and Politics*, 1: 42–66.

Kahn, R.L. and Antonucci, T.C. (1980) Convoys over the life-course: attachment, roles and social support, in P. Baltes and O. Brim (eds) *Life Span Development and Behaviour, Vol. 3*. New York: Academic Press.

Kellett, P. and Moore, J. (2003) Routes to home: homelessness and home-making in contrasting societies, *Habitat International*, 27: 123–41.

Kertzer, David (1997) The proper role of culture in demographic explanation, in G.W. Jones, R.M. Douglas, J.C. Caldwell and R.M. d'Souza (eds) *The Continuing Demographic Transition*. Oxford: Clarendon Press.

Keynon, L. (1999) A home from home: students' transitional experiences of home, in T. Chapman and J. Hockey (eds) *Ideal Homes? Social Change and Domestic Life*. London: Routledge, pp. 84–95.

Kiernan, K. (1992) The impact of family disruption in childhood on transitions made in young adult life, *Population Studies*, 46: 213–24.

Kiernan, K. (2004) Unmarried cohabitation and parenthood in Britain and Europe, *Law and Policy*, 26: 33–55.

Kohli, M. (1999) Private and public transfers between generations: linking the family and the state, *European Societies*, 1: 81–104.

Korosec-Serfaty, P. (1985) Experience and the use of dwelling, in I. Altman and C. M. Werner (eds) *Home Environments*. London: Plenum Press, pp. 65–86.

Korosec-Serfaty, P. (1995) The home from attic to cellar, in L. Groat (ed.) *Giving Places Meanings*. London: Academic Press, pp. 257–76.

La Fontaine, J. (1986) An anthropological perspective on children in social worlds, in M. Richards and P. Light (eds) *Children of Social Worlds: Development in a Social Context*. Cambridge, MA: Harvard University Press.

Lasch, C. (1977) *Haven in a Heartless World*. New York: Basic Books.

Lee, N. (2001) *Children and Society: Growing Up in an Age of Uncertainty*. Buckingham: Open University Press.

Lefebvre, H. (1991) *The Production of Space*. Oxford: Basil Blackwell.

Leonard, D. (1980) *Sex and Generation*. London: Tavistock.

Leonard, M. (2001) Old wine in new bottles? Women working inside and outside the household, *Women's Studies International Forum*, 24: 67–78.

Levitt, P. and Waters, M. C. (eds) (2002) *The Changing Face of Home: The Transnational Lives of the Second Generation*. New York: Russell Sage Foundation.

Luescher, K. and Pillemer, K. (1998) Intergenerational ambivalence: a new approach to the study of parent-child relations in later life, *Journal of Marriage and the Family*, 60: 413–25.

MacDonald, R. and Marsh, J. (2001) Disconnected youth? *Journal of Youth Studies*, 4: 373–91.

MacDonald, R., Mason, P., Shildrick, T., Webster. C., Johnston, L. and Ridley, L. (2001) Snakes and ladders: in defence of studies of youth transition, *Sociological Research Online*, 5 (4). See http://www.socresonline.org.uk/5/4/macdonald.html.

Madigan, R., Munro, M. and Smith, S. J. (1990) Gender and the meaning of home, *International Journal of Urban and Regional Research*, 14: 625–47.

Marini, M.M. (1984) Age and sequencing norms in the transition to adulthood, *Social Forces*, 63: 229–44.

Mason, J. (1999) Living away from relatives: kinship and geographical reasoning, in S. McRae (ed.) *Changing Britain: Families and Households in the 1990s*. Oxford: Oxford University Press, pp. 156–75.

Massey, D. (1992) A place called home, *New Formations*, 17: 3–15.

McDowell, L. (2003) *Redundant Masculinities? Employment Change and White Working Class Youth*. Oxford: Blackwell.

McKendrick, J. (2004) Fallacies surrounding the geography of family eating, *Children's Geographies*, 2: 293–5.

Mead, G. (1934) *Mind, Self and Society*. Chicago: University of Chicago Press.

Merrifield, A. (2000) Henri Lefebvre: a socialist in space, in M. Crang and N. Thrift (eds) *Thinking Space*. London: Routledge, pp. 167–82.

Merton, R.K. and Barber, E. (1963) Sociological ambivalence, in E.A. Tiryakian (ed.) *Sociological Theory, Values and Sociocultural Change*. New York: Free Press, pp. 91–120.

Miles, S. (2000) *Youth Lifestyles in a Changing World*. Buckingham: Open University Press.

Miller, D. (ed.) (2002) *Home Possessions: Material Cultures Behind Closed Doors*. Berg: Oxford.

Milligan, M. J. (1998) Interactional past and potential: The social construction of place attachment, *Symbolic Interaction*, 21: 1–33.

Mills, C. W. (1959) *The Sociological Imagination*. Harmondsworth: Penguin.

Mitchell, B., Wister, A. and Burch, T.K. (1989) The family environment and leaving the parental home, *Journal of Marriage and the Family*, 51: 605–13.

Modell, J., Furstenberg, F.F. (jnr), and Hershberg, T. (1976) Social change and transition to adulthood in historical perspective, *Journal of Family History*, 1: 7–32.

Molgat, M. (2002) Leaving home in Quebec: theoretical and social implications of (im)mobility among youth, *Journal of Youth Studies*, 5: 135–52.

Moore, J. (2000) Placing *home* in context, *Journal of Environmental Psychology*, 20: 207–17.

Morgan, D.H.J. (1996) Family practices, in E. Silva and C. Smart (eds) *The New Family?* London: Sage, pp. 13–30.

Morgan, D. (2004) Everyday life and family practices, in E.B. Silva and T. Bennett (eds) *Contemporary Culture and Everyday Life*. Durham: Sociology Press.

Morrow, V. (1999) Conceptualising social capital in relation to the wellbeing of children and young people: a critical review, *Sociological Review*, 47: 744–65.

Morrow, V. and Richards, M. (1996) *Transitions to Adulthood: A Family Affair?* York: Joseph Rowntree Foundation.

Mulder, C. and Wagner, M. (1998) First-time home-ownership in the family life-course: A West German-Dutch comparison, *Urban Studies*, 35: 687–714.

Murphy, M. and Wang, D. (1998) Family and sociodemographic influences in patterns of leaving home in postwar Britain, *Demography*, 35: 293–305.

Oinonen, E. (2003) Extended present, faltering future: family formation in the process of attaining adult status in Finland and Spain, *Young: Scandinavian Journal of Youth Research*, 11: 121–40.

Pahl, R. (2000) *On Friendship*. Cambridge: Polity Press.

Patiniotis, J. and Holdsworth, C. (2005) 'Seize that chance!': Leaving home and transitions to higher education, *Journal of Youth Studies* 8: 81–95.

Pickvance, C.G. and Pickvance, K. (1995) The role of family help in the housing decisions of young people, *Sociological Review*, 43(1): 123–49.

Pooley, C. and Turnbull, J. (2004) Migration from the parental home in Britain since the eighteenth century, in F. van Poppel, M. Oris and J. Lee (eds) *The Road to Independence*. Oxford: Peter Lang, pp. 375–402.

Popenoe, D. (1988) *Disturbing the Nest: Family Change and Decline in Modern Societies*. New York: A. de Gruyter.

Porteous, D. (1976) Home: the territorial core, *Geographical Review*, 66: 383–90.

Punch, S. (2001) Negotiating autonomy: childhoods in rural Bolivia, in L. Alanen and B. Mayall (eds) *Conceptualising Child-Adult Relations*. London: Routledge/Falmer.

Punch, S. (2002) Youth transitions and interdependent adult-child relations in rural Bolivia, *Journal of Rural Studies*, 18: 123–33.

Rapoport, A. (1969) *House, Form and Culture*. Prentice Hall: New Jersey.

Reay, D. (2004) 'It's all becoming a habitus': beyond the habitual use of habitus in educational research, *British Journal of Sociology of Education*, 24: 431–44.

Reher, D. S. (1998) Family ties in Western Europe: persistent contrasts, *Population and Development Review*, 24: 203–34.

Ribbens McCarthy, J., Edwards, R. and Gillies, V. (2003) *Making Families: Moral Tales of Parenting and Step-Parenting*. Durham: Sociology Press.

Richards, L. (1990) *Nobody's Home: Dreams and Realities in a New Suburb*. Oxford. Oxford University Press.

Riessman, C. K. (1993) *Narrative Analysis*. London: Sage.

Roberts, K. (1997) Structure and agency: the new youth research agenda, in J. Bynner, L. Chisholm and A. Furlong (eds) *Youth, Citizenship and Social Change in a European Context*. Aldershot: Ashgate.

Roberts, K. (2003) Changes and continuity youth transitions in Eastern Europe: lessons for Western sociology, *Sociological Review*, 51: 484–505.

Roberts, K. (2004) Education and the labour market: European and American models and their relevance for the new market economies. Paper presented at the Thirty-sixth Congress of the IIS, Beijing, July 2004.

Roberts, K., Osadchaya, G.I., Dsuzev, H.V., Gorodyanenko, V.G. and Tholen, J. (2002) 'Who succeeds and who flounders?' Young people in East Europe's new market economies, *Sociological Research Online*, 7(4): http://www.socresonline.org.uk/7/4/roberts.html.

Rosh White, N. (2002) 'Not under my roof': young people's experience of home, *Youth and Society*, 34: 214–31.

Rossi, A.S. and Rossi, P.H. (1990) *Of Human Bonding: Parent-Child Relations Across the Life-Course*. New York: Aldine de Gruyter.

Saile, D.G. (1985) The ritual establishment of the home, in I. Altman and C.M. Werner (eds) *Home Environments*. London: Plenum Press, pp. 87–112.

Schnaiberg, A. and Goldenberg, S. (1989) From empty nest to crowded nest: the dynamics of incompletely launched young adults, *Social Problems*, 36: 251–69.

Schneider, J. (2000) The increasing financial dependency of young people on their parents, *Journal of Youth Studies*, 3: 5–20.

Schürer, K. (2004) Leaving home in England and Wales, in F. van Poppel, M. Oris and J. Lee (eds) *The Road to Independence*. Oxford: Peter Lang, pp. 33–84.

Scott, J. (2000) Is it a different world to when you were growing up? Generational effects on social representations and child-rearing values, *British Journal of Sociology*, 51: 355–76.

Seeley, J.R., Sim, R.A. and Loosley, E.W. (1956) *Crestwood Heights: A Study of the Culture of Suburban Life*. Basic Books: New York.

Sennett, R. (2003) *Respect: The Formation of Character in an Age of Inequality*. Harmondsworth: Penguin.

Settersten, R.A. (1998) A time to leave home and a time never to return? Age constraints on the living arrangements of young adults, *Social Forces*, 76: 1373–400.

Shields, R. (1999) *Lefebvre, Love and Struggle*. London: Routledge.

Sibley, D. (1995) *Geographies of Exclusion*, London: Routledge.

Sixsmith, J. (1986) The meaning of home: an exploratory study of environmental experience, *Journal of Environmental Psychology*, 6: 281–98.

Sixsmith, A. and Sixsmith, J. (1991) Transitions to home in later life, *Journal of Architectural and Planning Research*, 8: 181–91.

Skeggs, B. (1997) *Formations of Class and Gender*. London: Sage.

Skelton, T. (2002) Research on youth transitions: some critical interventions, in M. Cieslik and G. Pollock (eds) *Young People in Risk Society*. Aldershot: Ashgate, pp. 100–16.

Smelser, N. J. (1980) Issues in the study of work and love in adulthood, in N.J. Smelser and E.H. Erikson (eds) *Themes of Work and Love in Adulthood*. London: Grant McIntyre Ltd.

Somerville, P. (1992) Homelessness and the meaning of home: rooflessness or root-lessness, *International Journal of Urban and Regional Research*, 16: 529–39.

Somerville, P. (1997) The social construction of home, *Journal of Architectural and Planning Research*, 14: 226–45.

Sopher, D. (1978) The structuring of space and place names and words for place, in D. Ley and M.S. Samuels (eds) *Humanistic Geography: Prospects and Problems*. London: Croom Helm, pp. 251–68.

Sopher, D. (1979) The landscape of home: myth, experience, social meaning, in W. Meinig (ed.) *The Interpretation of Ordinary Landscapes: Geographical Essays*. Oxford: Oxford University Press, pp. 129–49.

Sullivan, O. (2000) The division of domestic labour: twenty years of change? *Sociology*, 34: 437–56.

Suzuki, T. (2001) Leaving the parental household in contemporary Japan, *Review of Population and Social Policy*, 10: 23–35.

Swidler, A. (1980) Love and adulthood in American culture, in N.J. Smelser and E.H. Erikson (eds) *Themes of Work and Love in Adulthood*. London: Grant McIntyre.

Swidler, A. (1986) Culture in action: symbols and strategies, *American Sociological Review*, 51: 237–86.

Te Riele, K. (2004) Youth transition in Australia: challenging assumptions of linearity and choice, *Journal of Youth Studies*, 7: 243–57.

Thomson, R., Bell, R., Holland, J., Henderson, S., Mcgrellis, S. and Sharpe, S. (2002) Critical moments: choice, chance and opportunity in young people's narratives of transition, *Sociology*, 36: 335–54.

Thomson, R. and Holland, J. (2002) Imagining adulthood: resources, plans and contradictions, *Gender and Education*, 14: 337–50.

Tuan, Y. (1974) Space and place: humanistic perspective, *Progress in Human Geography*, 6: 211–52.

Urry, J. (2000) *Sociology Beyond Societies: Mobilities for the Twenty-First Century*. London: Routledge.

Valentine, G. (1999) 'Oh Please Mum. Oh Please Dad': Negotiating children's spatial boundaries, in L. McKie, S. Bowlby and S. Gregory (eds) *Gender, Power and the Household*. Basingstoke: Macmillan Palgrave, pp. 137–54.

Valentine, G. (2003) Boundary crossings: transitions from childhood to adulthood, *Children's Geographies*, 1: 37–52.

Van Poppel, F., Oris, M. and Lee, J. (eds) (2004) *The Road to Independence*. Oxford: Peter Lang.

Veevers, J.E. and Mitchell, B.A. (1998) Intergenerational exchanges and perceptions of support within 'boomerang kid' family environment, *International Journal of Aging and Human Development*, 46: 91–108.

Wall, R. (1978) The age at leaving home, *Journal of Family History*, 3: 181–202.

Wallace, C. and Kovatcheva, S. (1998) *Youth in Society: The Construction and Deconstruction of Youth in East and West Europe*. Basingstoke: Macmillan.

Weeks, J., Heaphy, B. and Donovan, C. (2001) *Same Sex Intimacies: Families of Choice and Other Life Experiments*. London: Routledge.

Werner, C. M., Altman, I. and Oxley, D. (1985) Temporal aspects of homes: a transactional perspective, in I. Altman and C. M. Werner (eds) *Home Environments*. London: Plenum Press, pp. 1–32.

Westberg, A. (2004) Forever young? Young people's conception of adulthood: the Swedish case, *Journal of Youth Studies*, 7: 35–53.

Whittington, L. and Peters, H.E. (1996) Economic incentives for financial and residential independence, *Demography*, 33: 82–97.

Williams, R. (1983) *Keywords: A Vocabulary of Culture and Society* (revised edn.). London: Flamingo.

Wood, D. and Beck, R.J. (1994) *Home Rules*. Baltimore: The Johns Hopkins University Press.

Yamaguchi, K. (1991) *Event History Analysis*. London: Sage.

Yi, Z., Coale, A., Choe, M.K., Zhiwu, L. and Li, L. (1994) Leaving the parental home: census-based estimates for China, Japan, South Korea, United States, France, and Sweden, *Population Studies*, 48: 65–80.

Author Index

Subject Index

Related books from Open University Press
Purchase from www.openup.co.uk or order through your local bookseller

HARD LABOUR
THE SOCIOLOGY OF PARENTHOOD, FAMILY LIFE AND CAREER

Caroline Gatrell

This book examines changes in family practices and paid work in the twenty-first century. Focusing principally on highly qualified women who combine the mothering of very young children with employment, it makes a valuable contribution to current debates. Unlike other books in the field, which focus on one gender only, this innovative book also takes into account the views of fathers, making it a rounded study of family practice in the new millennium.

The first part of *Hard Labour* provides an up-to-date, comprehensive and readable overview of the literature on motherhood, fatherhood, family practices, and women in employment. The second part draws on a qualitative study of the lives of 20 mothers and their husbands/partners, each of whom is educated to degree level or above, and has at least one child under five. Key aspects of the family lives of the men and women interviewed are considered, for example how they manage their commitments to one another, their children and their professional work, and how they share out family tasks such as childcare and housework. At each stage, the empirical research is explicitly placed in the context of the literature referenced in the first part, and of the wider debate on career motherhood.

This book is essential reading for students and academics in sociology, family policy, family studies, women's or gender studies and the sociology of management/ employment.

Contents
Part 1: The sociology of parenting and paid work – 'The impossible dream?' Motherhood and employment – Parents, children and family lives – 'Domestic Goddesses?' The sociology of motherhood in Britain and the USA – 'Moneybags' and the 'invisible' father – Working for love or money? The commitment of mothers to paid work – Part 2: Doing it all (and having some of it) – 'Baby, you changed my life': The transition to motherhood – A labour of love (and a sound investment) The division of childcare work and the centrality of children to fathers' lives – 'Everything I do, I do for you' The commitment to work and child – Everyone is equal . . .? Parenthood and workplace discrimination – 'My children must become our *children'.*

256pp   0 335 21488 6 (Paperback)   0 335 21489 4 (Hardback)

FAMILIES, VIOLENCE AND SOCIAL CHANGE

Linda McKie

In this innovative book, Linda McKie analyses violence among adults who are known to each other through intimate and family relationships. She examines the family as a changing institution and supposed haven from the public sphere of life, and uses case studies of domestic violence to develop a critical approach to sociological work on families and violence. She asks why policies and services so often focus on those experiencing rather than perpetrating violence, and contends that greater attention must be paid to the broader social, cultural and economic contexts that sanction and silence violence in families.

Topics include:

- Identifying and explaining violence in families
- Embodiment, gender and violence
- Older women and domestic violence
- How social and economic changes affect the family

The book draws upon a range of sociological theories and research and, in particular, theories that address the themes of cohesion and conflict, and studies of gender and violence.

Key reading for undergraduate students of the social sciences studying families, gender, health, criminology and the process and impact of social change.

Contents

Series editor's foreword – Acknowledgements – Introduction – Part one: Families, violence and society – Your family, my family, their family – Identifying and explaining – Families: Fusion and fission – Part two: Gender, age and violence – Embodied individuals, gender neutrality and families: the case of domestic violence – The contingencies and ambiguities of growing older: the case of elder abuse – Part three: Towards a critical theory – Conclusions: towards a critical social theory of families, violence and social change – References – Index.

c.192pp   0 335 21158 5 (Paperback)   0 335 21159 3 (Hardback)

Open up your options

 Education

Health & Social Welfare

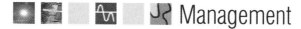 Management

Media, Film & Culture

Psychology & Counselling

Sociology

Study Skills

for more information on our
publications visit **www.openup.co.uk**

OPEN UNIVERSITY PRESS

McGraw - Hill Education